GOD IS IN THE

Hard STUFF

D1055070

GOD IS IN THE Hard STUFF

BRUCE & STAN

BARBOUR
PUBLISHING

This special edition of God Is in the Hard Stuff
*was printed for free distribution to Hurricane Katrina survivors
and is not intended for resale.*

Special thanks to Lake Book Manufacturing for its assistance with this project.

© 2005 by Bruce Bickel and Stan Jantz

ISBN 1-59789-286-6

All rights reserved. No part of this publication may be reproduced or transmitted for commercial purposes, except for brief quotations in printed reviews, without written permission of the publisher.

Churches and other noncommercial interests may reproduce portions of this book without the express written permission of Barbour Publishing, provided that the text does not exceed 500 words or 5 percent of the entire book, whichever is less, and that the text is not material quoted from another publisher. When reproducing text from this book, include the following credit line: "From *God Is in the Hard Stuff,* published by Barbour Publishing, Inc. Used by permission."

Unless otherwise indicated, all Scripture quotations are taken from the *Holy Bible,* New Living Translation, copyright © 1996. Used by permission of Tyndale House Publishers, Inc. Wheaton, Illinois 60189, U.S.A. All rights reserved.

Scripture quotations marked THE MESSAGE are from *THE MESSAGE.* Copyright © by Eugene H. Peterson 1993, 1994, 1995, 1996, 2000, 2001, 2002. Used by permission of NavPress Publishing Group.

Cover design by Lookout Design, Inc.

Published by Barbour Publishing, Inc., P.O. Box 719, Uhrichsville, Ohio 44683 www.barbourbooks.com

Our mission is to publish and distribute inspirational products offering exceptional value and biblical encouragement to the masses.

 Member of the
Evangelical Christian
Publishers Association

Printed in the United States of America.
5 4 3 2 1

Contents

INTRODUCTION

Before we go any further, we want to introduce ourselves. We're Bruce and Stan, two ordinary guys who care very much about the extraordinary and heartbreaking events that have affected so many people. We don't know you, but we know something about you. If you are a survivor of Hurricane Katrina's fury and the subsequent flooding, we know you are someone of great *courage*. You may not feel very courageous, but we know better. Even though you have experienced great loss, terrible pain, and constant uncertainty, you are still standing. That takes courage.

If you are reading this and you are involved in some kind of relief effort, we know you are a person of *compassion*. You weren't content to sit back and watch things happen. You saw a great need and you offered yourself unselfishly.

If you are neither a victim nor a caregiver, we still know that you are filled with *concern*. You care about what's going on. Perhaps you have contributed in some way, or you have offered your sincere prayers. You may not be able to get involved directly, but you are offering what you can.

So, in a sense, we *do* know you—and we know that whatever your situation is right now, you are facing some "hard stuff," perhaps the hardest of your life. The hurricane is just one—albeit a really big one—of the challenges of life. No doubt you are now dealing with hard stuff that affects your health, your employment, your relationships, and perhaps even your faith. You may have questions about where God is in all of these matters. You may wonder if He even cares.

While we don't have complete answers for all of life's hard stuff, we think there is a sensible way to approach the question. This special edition of *God Is in the Hard Stuff* contains forty short essays on a variety of difficult topics that we hope will give you a place to start when it comes to sorting out some of these tough things we all experience from time to time.

As you read through these chapters and the accompanying "proverbs" that offer suggestions on how to make sense of the hard stuff in your life, keep one important thing in mind: God loves you more than you can ever imagine. Even though you may not realize it right now, God knows what you are going through, and He knows how it feels to suffer.

Suffering of any kind is difficult, but it's nothing to be ashamed of. In fact, those who suffer gain a perspective on life and an appreciation for God that others do not have. While he was suffering in prison, the apostle Paul wrote, "I am not ashamed of it, for I know the one in whom I trust, and I am sure that he is able to guard what I have entrusted to him until the day of his return" (2 Timothy 1:12).

Our prayer for you is that you would entrust the hard stuff of your life to God, and that He would in turn reveal Himself to you in tangible ways as He strengthens you for the days ahead.

Bruce & Stan

You promised me, Lord, that if I followed You,
You would walk with me always.
But I have noticed that during
the most trying periods of my life
there has only been one set of footprints in the sand.
Why, when I needed You most,
have You not been there for me?"
The Lord replied, "The years when you have seen only
one set of footprints, My child, is when I carried you."

from "Footprints in the Sand"
Author anonymous

WHY, GOD, WHY?

When things are going well in your life, everything seems good with the world:

- The sun shines brighter.
- The flowers are more fragrant.
- People smile as they pass by you.
- There is a vacant parking spot for you directly in front of Starbucks.

Of course, things aren't really that way, but that's how they seem to you because you're feeling good about your situation.

When your circumstances turn south, though, there seems to be an odd confluence with the rest of the cosmos. Everything seems to sour simultaneously:

- You get soaking wet after being caught in a freak rain storm.
- You get a flat tire and don't have a jack in the trunk.
- Everyone who crosses your path is in a foul mood.
- After waiting fifteen minutes in the drive-thru at Starbucks, you are informed that they are out of coffee.

It's bad enough that [insert your tragedy here] happened to you—but to make things worse, it became a triggering mechanism for further misfortune.

These are trivial illustrations of how your perspective is corrupted when you are forced to endure a tragic circumstance or a particularly hard situation. But more than your attitude is affected by adversity. Your spiritual equilibrium can also be thrown off kilter. Often, the frustration that accompanies your hardship leads to a spiritual misconception: *God has abandoned you.* While this isn't true, it is easy to see how you can reach this flawed conclusion. First, you start with sound premises, such as:

- God is the almighty Creator and Ruler of the universe.
- All things are under His sovereign control.
- Nothing happens in the world without His knowledge or permission.
- God loves you and wants only what is best for you.

So far, your theology is on track. But here is the point where your logic slips a cog. You mistakenly conclude:

- Since tragedy has entered your life, God must have turned His back on you.
- If He really loved you, He wouldn't let this happen to you.

This line of thinking is flawed. First, God never promises anyone a life free from pain. So don't make the mistake of thinking that God has abandoned you when hardship enters your life. Secondly, the *presence of hardship* in your life does not imply the *absence of God* in your life. To the contrary, you can be sure that God is there and wants to reveal Himself to you when you are experiencing difficulties.

Rather than approaching your hard times with the attitude that God has vanished, use these circumstances to find God. He is there. And He isn't hiding. He wants you to feel His presence. He wants you to sense His love for you. He desires for you to understand His purposes for allowing these difficulties in your life.

God is with you. Yes, He is all-powerful and capable of changing the hard circumstances of your life. But because He loves you and wants what is best for you, He will not eliminate those problems if He knows they serve a beneficial purpose in your life. He never promised to protect you from all hurt, but He has promised to be by your side during every bit of it.

If you mistakenly assume that God is not present, you'll be spiritually blind to His presence. But if you take God at His word and expect to find Him in the darkest hours, you'll be surprised that you see Him all around you. Suddenly, the severity of your problems will shrink in comparison to the magnitude of God's presence in your life.

- God doesn't remove the difficulty and pain. But He will be there with you through it all.

- It is almost impossible to see God if your spiritual eyes are closed.

- God's continual presence with you is one of His presents to you.

- How do you expect to recognize God during times of crisis if you haven't been taking notice of Him when things are going well?

- God is with you when the going gets tough, but He's a perfect gentleman. He won't carry your load unless you ask Him to.

Complete success alienates
a man from his fellows,
but suffering makes kinsmen of us all.

Elbert Hubbard

TWO

INNOCENT SUFFERING

Of all the types of suffering we see in the world, the most difficult to understand is the suffering of the innocent—especially when it comes as the result of a natural calamity. When the fierce winds, rain, and floodwaters of Hurricane Katrina hit the Gulf Coast of the United States, it was hard to comprehend the magnitude of such suffering. After a while, the images coming through our televisions—homes splintered and scattered by the winds, streets filled with rising water, people clinging to rooftops for their very lives, and bodies floating amidst the debris—all blurred together, leaving many of us emotionally numb.

Then, perhaps, you saw a reporter interviewing a father who

had to let go of his wife in order to save his children. As he wept, your emotions began to well up—and in an instant a knot formed in your stomach. You hurt for this family and countless others whom you will never know, but somehow identify with. You are not related, yet you are connected by the common bond of humanity.

But maybe you didn't see the reports on television. Maybe you actually lived through the horror. You endured the storm's wrath. You witnessed the devastation and the loss of life. You looked into the eyes of a child who lost her mommy and daddy. For you, the images are burned into your memory like a series of cruel photographs, and you wonder how you will ever make sense of it all.

Whether you watched the holocaust of nature on television or experienced it personally, you can't help but feel a sense of helplessness. Because they originate on this planet we call home, we all feel the sting when the earth convulses and produces disasters like Hurricane Katrina. And we wonder: Can we trust this life-giving sphere that is usually so good to us? It all seems rather capricious, especially when those who are least able to handle the terrestrial blast of hurricanes, floods, and tsunamis—the poor and the disadvantaged—are often hit the hardest.

How do we deal with the suffering that inevitably comes from such a disaster? What are our options? We can believe that nature has run amok and out of God's control. Or we can believe that nature is all there is, with no God to care or wield any authoritative restraint. Those are the options of people who have given up on God. They aren't very comforting, are they? If nature is the beginning and the end of all things, and we are merely pawns in a mindless game of chance and natural selection (it's survival of the fittest, you know), then there is no need to wonder why we suffer—because there is no explanation.

People who still hold out for a belief in some kind of God—and most of the world operates this way—look beyond nature for answers. In this realm of belief, there are multiple views. One is that God is using nature to inflict punishment on His wayward created beings. He did it once—remember the Great Flood?—and He can do it again. Ah, but there's the rainbow, God's promise to humankind that he will never inflict such worldwide harm again:

> *"I will never again curse the earth, destroying all living things, even though people's thoughts and actions are bent toward evil from childhood. As long as the earth remains, there will be springtime and harvest, cold and heat, winter and summer, day and night."* GENESIS 8:21–22

We must look elsewhere for some kind of explanation, though none can be found to satisfy everyone. Perhaps a partial answer is found in the New Testament. In his letter to the first-century Roman church, the apostle Paul wrote:

> *All creation anticipates the day when it will join God's children in glorious freedom from death and decay. For we know that all creation has been groaning as in the pains of childbirth right up to the present time.*
>
> ROMANS 8:21–22

Even creation is under the weight of sin and suffering, brought into this world by rebellious acts of the people God made. It isn't that God has lost control; He is merely allowing His creation to operate in the physical world He made for us, functioning superbly and incredibly 99.9 percent of the time. Occasionally, though, it groans from the contractions that will someday result in a new heaven and a new earth.

We may never understand the reason why God allows these things to happen, but we can take comfort in the fact that He is still in control, still offering His mighty hand to those who put their trust in Him. The psalmist David writes:

> *The LORD rules over the floodwaters. The LORD reigns as king forever. The LORD gives his people strength. The LORD blesses them with peace.* PSALM 29:10–11

Meanwhile, just as nature groans, we must also groan—with compassion—for those affected by Earth's sometimes unexplainable behavior. If we are to find meaning in any of this, we must find it in the help we can give to those who suffer.

. . .In the Hard Stuff

- People without God are people without hope.

- This world is an imperfect place, but it is the best of all possible worlds.

- God has taken extraordinary measures to provide a comfortable and beneficial place for us to live.

- God does not *cause* suffering, but He *allows* it to happen for reasons we don't always understand.

- Never allow your own comfort to keep you from giving comfort to others.

It is easier to bear some abuse if I reflect,
"I do not deserve this reproach but
I do deserve others that have not been made."

Francois Mauriac

THREE

WHEN LIFE DOESN'T SEEM FAIR

No one likes hard times, but difficulties are even tougher to take if their imposition seems unfair. There appear to be three levels for determining whether hardship is deserved or undeserved:

- LEVEL 1—*I deserve it.* Much of the time, we can't blame the devil—or God—for the problems that enter our lives. Often those difficult circumstances are just the natural and inevitable result of our poor choices or foolish behavior.

- LEVEL 2—*I don't deserve it, but it's a part of life.* We live in a broken world, with rampant evil, illness, and natural disasters. No one is immune from misfortune. If you are hoping to avoid trouble, the odds are against you. As a resident of planet Earth, sooner or later it is going to get you.
- LEVEL 3—*I was doing something good, and this is the thanks I get?* Sometimes trouble comes your way when you're being nice to someone else or engaged in a good cause.

At Level 1, bad things happen to bad people; your struggles are compensatory—you brought them on yourself. At Level 2, bad things happen to good people; your strife is undeserved, but at least it is understandable, so you endure it. But Level 3 is the hardest to rationalize; this is when bad things happen to good people when they are doing good things.

It doesn't seem right that undeserved grief should be heaped upon you when you are engaged in a noble effort. But it happens:

- You stand up for a coworker who is unjustly criticized, and you lose your job for insubordination.
- You have been caring for an infirm parent for many years. It has been a thankless and exhausting job. To protect your own sanity and provide better care at a critical stage, you make the difficult decision to opt for a nursing home. Your adult siblings, all of whom live out-of-state and have never offered any assistance, accuse you of being selfish and heartless.
- You take the right stand on a black-and-white moral issue, but the offending party manipulates the situation and *you become the bad guy*.

Here is the irony of it all. You got involved only because you are a good person. Anyone with less character would have remained on the sidelines; the spineless ones are safe and unscathed. But because of your integrity, you were compelled to enter the fray. You were willing to sacrifice time and energy and emotion. In light of what you were willing to give—which others were not—you should have gotten a reward. Instead, you gained nothing but undeserved grief.

But you didn't engage in your noble act for the sake of a reward. You did it because it was the right thing to do. And that's the perspective you need to maintain when you suffer for doing good. God honors those who do what is right. He has mercy on those who are defenseless. You can thank God that He has wired you in such a way that you cannot stand idly by in the face of injustice or wrongdoing. If God created you to take a stand for the cause of right, you can be assured that He will rescue you from the accompanying fallout.

- No good deed goes unpunished.

- Sometimes the criticism of others affirms the propriety of your action.

- Those who don't have the courage to respond often have the nerve to complain.

- If God gives you strength of character, He will also give you skin thick enough to repel the sticks and stones of criticism.

- Integrity means doing what is right, even when it isn't popular. Popularity allows you to live with others, but integrity lets you live with yourself.

There's something about resurrections
that requires crosses.

Robert Sloan

FOUR

WHERE IS GOD WHEN WE SUFFER?

It's so easy to shake our fists at God when something extraordinarily painful happens to us. The most natural question to ask is, "Where is God in all of this?" Maybe you have asked, *Where is God in my cancer? Where is God in my father's stroke? Where is God in my baby's birth defect?*

Maybe you've asked the question in less physical situations that are no less painful. You could be going through a nasty divorce. One of your children could be disrupting your entire household through his or her poor choices. Or you could be the victim of corporate downsizing, creating an unbearable financial strain. Where is God in all of this? Hasn't He promised an abundant life to His children?

Doesn't He care when we hurt?

Yes, God does care. He cares so much that it cost Him the life of His only Son. You see, when we think that God neither cares about us nor identifies with our suffering and hurts, we forget that the Son of God suffered beyond what any of us can even imagine. From the beginning of His ministry on earth, Jesus knew what He had to do: bear the cumulative sin and sickness and evil and disease and pain of the entire human race. This was the incredible burden Jesus carried. It was His mission, and He knew it (Matthew 16:21).

No wonder, then, that when Jesus was praying in the Garden of Gethsemane He asked the Father to release Him from the terrible task at hand. "Yet I want your will, not mine," He said (Matthew 26:39). We know that God's will was for Jesus to suffer and die so that we would have the opportunity to live. We may not understand it, but suffering—most significantly the suffering of Christ—is God's way of fixing what went wrong when sin entered and nearly destroyed the world.

When we ask, "Where is God when we suffer?" we need only look to Christ, who suffered for us so that ultimately, in the life that follows this temporal existence, we won't have to suffer. Meanwhile, we live imperfectly in an imperfect world. We see through a glass darkly, knowing that someday our tears and pain will be removed. . .for good. When we do suffer—as long as we aren't suffering for something that comes from our own poor choices—we can take comfort in knowing that we are "partners with Christ" in His suffering (1 Peter 4:13).

As people who walk this earth with a heavenly perspective, suffering is both our curse and our calling. We may not like it or understand why, but we know there is Someone who has gone before us and promises never to leave us.

. . .In the Hard Stuff

- Never forget that God knows firsthand what it's like to suffer.

- God's will is not always the easiest, but it is always the best.

- Sometimes God chooses the most unlikely methods to accomplish His purposes.

- Any good we experience comes from God.

- Any good we experience here on earth will pale in comparison to what awaits us in eternity.

Lord, on You I call for help
against my blind and senseless torment,
since You alone can renew
inwardly and outwardly my mind,
my will, and my strength, which are weak.

Michelangelo

YOU'RE NOT EXEMPT

There are certain privileges that accompany association:

- If you are a member of AAA, you get hotel discounts.
- If you are affiliated with an airline's frequent flyer club, you accumulate bonus miles for free travel.
- If you work at McDonald's, you might get to eat the French fries left over at closing time.
- If you are a sales clerk at J.C. Penney, you get

an employee discount on clothing.

- If your spouse is in law enforcement, the highway patrol officer might let you off with a warning when you've been doing eighty m.p.h. in a seventy zone.

Many people think there are comparable "exclusive membership benefits" if they associate with God. They think there is some providential protection that surrounds everyone who believes in Him. They believe a guardian angel guarantee will protect them from trouble, tragedy, and turmoil. Too bad for them—they must not have read the fine print in their celestial contract.

The fact that God does not insulate those He loves from pain and suffering should be evident. For example, consider Jesus—who had a *very* close association with God. God allowed Jesus to suffer. And if you are unclear about that, just watch Mel Gibson's movie *The Passion of the Christ*. (The word *passion* used in this context refers to suffering.) But Jesus wasn't alone in His suffering. According to ancient tradition, most of His close followers endured torture and/or a painful death:

- Stephen and Matthew were martyred.
- Luke and Philip were both hanged.
- Peter and Simeon were crucified.
- Mark was dragged to his death in the streets of Alexandria.
- John was dunked into a pot of boiling water.
- Bartholomew was killed by having his skin ripped off while he was still alive.

All of these men loved God. But if you were God's P.R. agent, these are not the stories you would put in a recruiting brochure. Their treatment runs contrary to our notion that God shelters those He loves from harm. Well, that notion is flat-out wrong. Our tendency is to decorate our concepts of God with thoughts of love and peace and "blessings." It's true that God is about all those things. But that is a limited and one-dimensional understanding of His nature. We must expand our understanding of God—including a realization that He considers troubles to be a blessing. That's why the Bible says we are to rejoice when hardships come our way:

Dear brothers and sisters, whenever trouble comes your
way, let it be an opportunity for joy. For when your
faith is tested, your endurance has a chance to grow. So
let it grow, for when your endurance is fully developed,
you will be strong in character and ready for anything.

JAMES 1:2–4

God doesn't want us to rejoice in suffering simply because He has a perverse sense of humor. He wants us to realize that our struggles drive us closer to Him. Difficulties are a necessary component for building the foundation of our faith. They cause us to seek God, because we might otherwise tend to ignore Him in tranquil circumstances. They impress upon us our need for God. They expose our lack of self-sufficiency, and we become convinced of our dependency on Him.

The next time difficulties come your way, don't say, "I love God. . .this shouldn't be happening to me." Instead, realize that those circumstances haven't escaped God's notice. He loves you and can use such situations for your good.

- Easy times may make you spiritually indifferent, but hard times make you spiritually dependent. And that is exactly how God wants you.

- Satan wants your life to be easy, but God loves you too much to allow that to happen.

- Loving God doesn't exempt you from troubles, but it does ensure that you can find meaning and purpose in them.

- Loving God doesn't exempt you from troubles, but it does ensure that you won't go through them alone.

- The Bible says to rejoice in your troubles. That means that when life gets bad, you've still got something good going on.

Yet what we suffer now
is nothing compared to
the glory he will give us later.

Romans 8:18

SIX

THANKING GOD

Is it possible to thank God when we hurt? Is it possible to thank God when we observe the suffering of others? Not only is it possible, it's advisable. When we fail to acknowledge God in our suffering, we fail to understand why we are able to get through it.

You may not feel like thanking God in the midst of your suffering, and certainly you don't want to thank God when a disaster strikes someone else but misses you. That's not what we're talking about. Thanking God when we hurt goes much deeper.

Thanking God in our suffering means that we can thank Him for getting us *through* our suffering. Have you ever been surprised by how much pain you can endure? When you were very young, it didn't take much to make you cry. A pinched finger or an unkind word was usually enough to get the tears flowing. But through the years you have toughened up. You can handle more pain, especially if it means helping to ease the pain of someone else.

The apostle Paul experienced more than his share of pain and suffering. He was beaten on many occasions, shipwrecked, and thrown in prison several times. Once Paul was bitten by a poisonous snake! He didn't ignore or try to minimize his problems; Paul was very aware of the trials he had endured. Even more, he was aware of his resilience in the face of overwhelming odds. In his letter to the Corinthian church, he wrote:

> *We are pressed on every side by troubles, but we are*
> *not crushed and broken. We are perplexed, but we don't*
> *give up and quit. We are hunted down, but God never*
> *abandons us. We get knocked down, but we get up*
> *again and keep going.*   2 CORINTHIANS 4:8–9

Paul's determination reminds us of Winston Churchill, whose most famous speech was also his shortest and most powerful. As Adolf

Hitler was threatening to overrun England and Western Europe, Churchill said to a group of students:

> *Never give in—never, never, never, never, in nothing great or small, large or petty, never give in except to convictions of honour and good sense. Never yield to force; never yield to the apparently overwhelming might of the enemy.*

No doubt there have been times when you gritted your teeth and snarled in the face of adversity. Where does this determination come from? It can come from only one source—our Creator, who built into every person the strength to overcome adversity.

Like Paul, we may feel crushed and broken—but we aren't! We may not know why certain things are happening to us, but we don't give up. We can thank God for what many have called the indomitable human spirit. And we can thank God for never, ever abandoning us.

There's another sense in which we can thank God in our suffering. When things get so bad that we don't think we can bear it any longer, there is someone we can count on to help ease our burden.

His name is Jesus, the one who suffered for us more than we will ever know. He is the one who makes our life possible.

Jesus once spoke to a group of people, many of whom were just like us—burdened and hurting. He offered words of comfort that are just as real now as they were two thousand years ago:

> *"Come to me, all of you who are weary and carry heavy burdens, and I will give you rest. Take my yoke upon you. Let me teach you, because I am humble and gentle, and you will find rest for your souls. For my yoke fits perfectly, and the burden I give you is light."*
>
> MATTHEW 11:28–30

God has made you to endure and overcome suffering, and Jesus promises to help carry your heavy load. That's why we can be thankful in our suffering.

- Thanking God in everything will help you get through anything.

- Never take delight in the misfortune of others.

- Everyone's pain threshold is different. Be sensitive—not critical—with someone who is more sensitive to pain than you are.

- Your ability to handle adversity comes from the God who has overcome adversity.

- God will never, never, never, never abandon you.

Job stood up and tore his robe in grief.
Then he shaved his head and fell to the ground before God.
He said, "I came naked from my mother's womb,
and I will be stripped of everything when I die.
The LORD gave me everything I had,
and the LORD has taken it away.
Praise the name of the LORD!"
In all of this, Job did not sin by blaming God.

Job 1:20–22

SEVEN

THE STORY OF JOB

It was a cosmic challenge that occurred approximately four thousand years ago. Satan alleged that Job was a faithful follower of God only because God had blessed Job with great prosperity. God knew better, but He allowed Satan to "test" Job by intervening in the circumstances of Job's life and decimating his idyllic situation. Unbeknownst to him, Job was about to endure a real-life riches-to-rags drama. Literally within moments, Job received news that

- a band of desert marauders had stolen his oxen and donkeys and killed his farmhands;

- all of his sheep and shepherds were killed in a freak fire storm;
- raiders had stolen his camels and murdered his servants;
- a fierce windstorm caused the collapse of a house that killed all of his sons and daughters.

To add further distress in Job's time of grief, Satan struck him with festering boils from his head to his feet. But in all of this tragedy, Job did not blame God.

Job's wife found him sitting in a pile of rubble and ashes, scraping his sores with a piece of broken pottery. While theologians through the ages have criticized her for a lack of faith in God's sovereignty, she seemed to respond with natural, human emotions when she yelled at Job, saying, "Are you still maintaining an allegiance to God? Get over it. Just curse God and die!" (see Job 2:9).

At this point in the story we learn a valuable lesson from Job. He disclosed to his wife a perspective on life—the perspective of how he could worship God in the midst of adversity with the same intensity and reverence that he had during times of prosperity:

"Should we accept only good things from the hand of God and never anything bad?" JOB 2:10

This question is simply profound, and profoundly simple: It is easy to trust God with the oversight of our lives when we are enjoying the ride. But shouldn't we also trust Him when the going gets hard? Even when it gets *very hard*? After all, doesn't God know what we need in our lives to achieve His purposes? Why do we suppose that He should be restricted to using only pleasant circumstances?

Like Job's wife, we often make the mistake of constructing a paradigm that assumes God can work in our lives only through prosperity. Job saw through that faulty logic. If we anticipate (and desire) that God is accomplishing His will in our lives, then we must factor into our life's equation the *ways* in which God works. Those ways are many and varied. He works through His Word, the Bible. He works through other people. And He can work through any succession of enjoyable circumstances, from the mundane to the miraculous: a salary increase, moving into a new home, a reconciled relationship, the birth of a baby, or the recovery from a significant health problem.

But God's way may also include a succession of unpleasant events, even catastrophes: the loss of a job, the foreclosure on your home, a breakup of a valued relationship, the birth of a deformed child, or the diagnosis of a fatal disease.

Like Job, we need to come into a deeper understanding of how God works. When we appreciate that God uses the hard stuff in our lives, it will make those circumstances easier to endure. But that isn't the entire benefit of Job's perspective. There is the added bonus that we will begin to see God at work in those difficult situations. All of a sudden, life's challenges aren't simply something to be endured. We can begin to see them as tools God is using to shape our lives for the better—and we can see God as the Master Craftsman skillfully using those tools to shape us according to His design. That's why after Job had endured more suffering than most of us could ever conceive, he was able to say to God:

> *"I had heard about you before, but now I have seen you with my own eyes."* JOB 42:5

- God's best for you may not always be your preference.

- Try to see God in the hard stuff with the same clarity that you see Him in the fun stuff.

- Have you only *heard* about God, or have you really *seen* Him?

- You can curse God and die, or you can find a reason for living in what He brings your way.

- Don't let the secret of Job's life go undiscovered in your life.

Happiness is not a reward—
it is a consequence.
Suffering is not a punishment—
it is a result.

Robert Green Ingersoll

EIGHT

THE SECRET OF JOB

The book of Job seems to discourage those who offer easy answers for why we suffer. Three of Job's friends—Eliphaz, Bildad, and Zophar—came to visit Job, and when they saw him in his miserable state, they didn't know what to say. But then, one by one, they told Job that his own sin had caused his suffering. They advised him to confess his sin and turn to God.

Have you ever felt that way—that your sin has somehow caused you to experience pain and heartache? It's true that our own sinful choices can lead to suffering, but more often than not that is no explanation at all. Just look around you. Some of the most sinful people seem to enjoy pain-free lives (at least from our perspective), while some of the most innocent and God-fearing people seem to bear more than their share of hard stuff.

Such was the case with Job. If ever there were an innocent and faithful person, it was Job. Yet he suffered as much as anyone in history. So how did Job handle his misery? For one thing, Job wisely refused to heed the advice of his friends and their simplistic answers. Instead, he turned to God. Whereas Job's friends tried to use human wisdom to answer the question of why we suffer (and did a very bad job of it), Job turned to the source of wisdom. There he found his answer.

If you think God gave Job a reason for his suffering, you're going to be disappointed. Rather than a reason, what God gave Job was hope. God reminded Job that He was the one who created the universe and everything in it. "Do you know the laws of the universe and how God rules the earth?" He asked Job.

Who are we to question God's justice and fairness? God is the standard of justice, and whatever He does is fair—even if we don't understand. Like Job, we need to trust God and remain faithful to Him, knowing that He sees the big picture and will never let go of us.

It's easy to answer the question of suffering by saying, like Job's friends, that it is God's judgment for sin. But this isn't always the case. Or we can conclude that God uses suffering to discipline and correct us. While this is sometimes true, it doesn't apply in every situation. The only satisfying answer is that suffering causes us to trust God for who He is. If we do that—and worry less about what God does—then we, like Job, will remain faithful to God, even when we don't understand.

. . .IN THE HARD STUFF

- The worst thing you can do to someone in distress is to offer advice.

- The best thing you can do is to listen and encourage.

- There's nothing to be gained by judging someone whose poor choices have led to suffering.

- There's everything to be gained by watching your own choices.

- Suffering is beneficial only if it helps you take your eyes off yourself and put them on God.

Prayer is not conquering God's reluctance,
but taking hold of God's willingness.

Phillips Brooks

NINE

WHEN PRAYER
DOESN'T SEEM TO WORK

Satan often plays an insidious trick on people of faith. During times of difficulty in their lives, he gets them to wonder whether their prayers to God have any effect. Consider how this ploy can escalate your feelings of discouragement and despair:

- You are already dealing with challenging struggles in your life. You come to the point where you are at the end of your resources. God is your only help.

- If heaven-sent relief doesn't come immediately, you begin to wonder whether your prayers are hitting the ceiling and stopping there. Even if they blast through the insulation in the attic and reach God, is He paying attention to them?

- If God is the only answer to your problem, and if He isn't being attentive to your situation, then it seems to you that you are doomed.

- So, in addition to the misery you are enduring, you now become spiritually despondent. With a fatalistic attitude, you simply give up. At precisely the time you should be praying the most, you stop all conversations with God because prayer seems to be an exercise in futility.

In circumstances such as this, the fault is not God's. The ineffectiveness of our prayers is often the fault of our own misunderstanding of the nature of God. To state it more succinctly: With bad theology, we pray in vain.

The essence of effective prayer is determined by our concept of who we are praying to. If we are praying to an all-knowing, all-loving, and all-powerful God, then His response will make sense. But if we are praying to a puny God, then it is no wonder that His replies seem useless to us.

When our prayer life falters, a false impression of God is frequently the culprit. We are not fully convinced of

- *His love.* Does God really care about me? Am I important to Him? There are so many people who are better than I am, so why would God love me?

- *His power.* Is God able to solve the problems I'm experiencing? Is He capable of intervening in all of the complicated, interconnected circumstances of my life to fully rectify the difficulties? My situation requires more than a quick fix; is God really up to the task?

- *His wisdom.* Does God know what is best for me? I'm in the middle of it, and I'm not even sure of the solution. Can I trust God's judgment? What if His opinion of what is best doesn't match with mine?

If you could be objective—looking at these issues without the pressure of present adversity in your life—you would know the answers to these questions. But, understandably, current misfortune has knocked your theology off track. So let's put the misconceptions to rest: The Bible says that God's love, power, and wisdom are infinite; they are perfect, and they are all focused on you. But if you doubt any of them, your prayers are hindered—not because God is rendered ineffective, but because you are not adequately prepared to accept His response.

Disappointment in prayer is usually caused by our failure to believe that He loves us, that He is fully capable of handling the circumstances of our lives, or that He knows what is best for us.

If your prayers have seemed ineffective, don't give up on prayer—and don't give up on God. Realize that you hold the top position on His "to do" list. Know that He is able to do exceedingly more than you can imagine. And finally, trust Him; acknowledge that His wisdom is greater than yours. His resolution of the situation may be different than what you expect—in timing and results—but it will be better than what you have in mind.

What are you waiting for? Give prayer another chance. But this time, properly consider the One to whom you are praying.

- If your prayers aren't working, make sure you are praying to the God who is all-loving, all-powerful, and all-knowing.

- Pray for the specific results that you want. Accept the results that God accomplishes.

- Don't expect God to answer your prayers if you don't really believe He can do anything about them.

- There is a time and place for prayer: anytime and anyplace.

- Prayer is a conversation between you and God; remember to do as much listening as you do talking.

In His will is our peace.

Dante Alighieri

TEN

HOW TO KNOW GOD'S WILL

What if you could know God's will for your life—from beginning to end? What if you could know in advance the best school to attend, or the right job to take, or the perfect person to marry? Life would be so much easier, right? Not necessarily. In fact, knowing in advance—and in every detail— what God wants you to do might just scare you to death!

You would know about all this great stuff God has in mind for you, and it might seem incredible. Or you would know about the hard stuff God will allow you to go through, and it might seem impossible. Either way, you might forget that God delights in doing the incredible, and you might not remember that He has promised to get you through the impossible—leading you to play it safe the rest of your life.

Of course, that's not what God wants for you. He doesn't want you to play it safe. God wants more for you than you could possibly want for yourself:

> *"No eye has seen, no ear has heard, and no mind has*
> *imagined what God has prepared for those who love*
> *him."*   1 CORINTHIANS 2:9

Even though you don't know exactly what God has prepared for you, you can be sure He has your best interest in mind. Meanwhile, you don't have to be completely in the dark when it comes to knowing God's will. And that means you can trust Him in good times and bad, when you're rich and when you're poor, when you're healthy and when you're sick. God doesn't change just because your circumstances do.

Never forget that God knows you better than you know yourself, and He knows what's best for you. God knows your weaknesses, and He knows your strengths. God knows your fears, and He knows your hopes. God will never mislead you or do you harm.

"For I know the plans I have for you," says the LORD.
*"They are plans for good and not for disaster, to give
you a future and a hope."*

JEREMIAH 29:11

Try to see things from God's perspective. When you insist on seeing God's will from *your* perspective, then your main concern is *doing* stuff for God. You get caught up in your own performance. By contrast, when you see God's will from His perspective, you are more concerned about *being*. Sure, God wants you to do stuff for Him, but He's more interested in the kind of person you are *becoming* than the specific things you are *doing*. He knows that when your *being* is right, your *doing* will be right, and you will be doing more things that please Him.

Commit yourself to the will of God. This means trusting that God has your best interests in mind at all times. Trusting God for your future—whether that future is tomorrow or ten years from now—begins with trusting God *now*. Once you have committed to doing God's will—regardless of what it is and what it costs—God will guide you every step of the way.

Trust in the LORD *with all your heart; do not depend on your own understanding. Seek his will in all you do, and he will direct your paths.*　PROVERBS 3:5–6

- The best thing about God's will is that it is always the best.

- God doesn't love you for what you do; He loves you for who you are.

- That being said, God loves it when you do what He wants you to do.

- Finding God's will should be satisfying, not frustrating.

- Don't wait for God to do something before you trust Him. Trust Him first, and then watch Him work.

By his [God's] mighty power at work within us,
he is able to accomplish infinitely
more than would ever dare to ask or hope.

Ephesians 3:20

ELEVEN

Trusting God

Let's get one thing straight: *God is God and you are not.* Okay, we don't expect much disagreement over that point.

The equally non-controversial corollary to that point is: *God knows more about anything and everything than you know.* Once again, we don't expect you to protest.

But here is the inevitable extension of that line of thinking: *God knows more about you than you know about yourself.* Are we starting to hit a nerve yet?

What about this? *God knows what character traits need to be developed in your life.* Have we finally reached a level of intimacy that you consider personally intrusive?

Self-improvement is an admirable goal. But did you ever stop to consider that we usually want to acquire the type of character traits that are associated with a life of ease and prosperity?

- We want to learn *generosity*—which implies that we'll have so much wealth we can afford to give some to others.
- We want to develop *humility*—which means that we first must achieve greatness in order to have something to be humble about.
- We want to be known for *gratefulness*—which suggests that God, through people and circumstances, has been so kind to us we should respond with appreciation.
- We want to reflect a tranquil spirit of *contentment*—which supposes that we have a fret-free life of ease.

But what if God determines that we need to develop an entirely different set of character traits? And what if the character set He has in mind can be forged in our lives only through adversity? What if He knows we need character values such as the following?

- *Patience.* Staying calm without complaining when the need is urgent but the solution is not yet a reality. The problem with *patience* is that it is only developed in desperate times.
- *Endurance.* The ability to bear prolonged pain or hardship. You enjoy prosperity; adversity must be endured. Thus, the precedent to endurance is tragedy and misfortune.
- *Forgiveness.* Graciously excusing an offense that was committed against us. If everyone is always nice and polite to you, then you'll have no chance to forgive. Your only chance at developing forgiveness is to take a few harsh, undeserved shots from others.
- *Integrity.* Sticking to your moral principles even when it means you will suffer unjust adverse circumstances. There is no ethical dilemma if there is no downside. Integrity is forged only in

the furnace of criticism and consequences.

- *Honesty.* Being truthful when it is the difficult and unpopular thing to do. Honesty comes naturally if praise and rewards are involved. But you develop honesty only in those tough times when it would be much easier to avoid the truth.

If you think you know what is best for yourself, then you can design your life any way you want it. Pick and choose those character traits that require no effort or discomfort (you might want to try starting with "sloth" and "selfishness"). But if you truly believe that God knows what is best for you, then you can't pick and choose by disregarding what is important to Him. Some of the character traits in His grand design can be achieved in your life only through harsh conditions.

* Learn to welcome what God is doing *in* your life by accepting the adversity He brings *to* your life.

* You'll never get better if you only pursue a life that is easier.

* Tough times won't break you; they will make you.

* God doesn't design hardship to make you fall flat; but He does hope that you'll be brought to your knees.

* The character traits worth having are those you acquired at the cost of personal sacrifice.

———————

This son of mine was dead
and has now returned to life.
He was lost, but now he is found."

———————

Luke 15:24

TWELVE

WHEN CHILDREN TURN AWAY

There are those children every parent dreams of having: they are respectful, loving, successful, and ambitious. Then there are those children parents actually have: disrespectful, petulant, stubborn, and lazy. You may not be a parent, but trust us—having kids is no picnic. Sure, parenthood has its share of thrills and unexpected joy, but it can also include overwhelming heartache and sorrow.

Thankfully, most kids grow out of those periods of rebellion that seem to foam and fester during the teenage years, paving the way for those glory years when, as adult children, they establish satisfying and meaningful relationships with their parents (and may even deliver a parent's greatest joy—grandchildren!). But there are situations in some families when it seems as though a wayward child will never return. Maybe that's where you are right now. Perhaps you are the parent of a child who has turned away and shows no signs of turning back.

You have done all you can, and yet it never seems enough. Some days you weep for your child, and other days anger fills your eyes with tears. Can you handle any more grief? Will things ever change? Is there any hope?

The short answer for all three of these questions is *yes*. You can handle it, things will change, and there is hope. How do we know? God has promised it. Whether you're dealing with a wayward child or some other heartbreaking situation, God has promised to see you through.

No test or temptation that comes your way is beyond the course of what others have had to face. All you need to remember is that God will never let you down; he'll never let you be pushed past your limit; he'll always be there to help you come through it.

1 CORINTHIANS 10:13 THE MESSAGE

No matter how dark the night, there is always the dawn. No matter how strong the storm, there will always be a calm. Things will change. That's not to say that your wayward child will change. There's no guarantee of that, because your children, despite your best efforts, must make their own choices and accept responsibility for them. Your child may not have a change of heart, but the experience will change yours.

At the same time, no matter how long you wait for things to turn around, always hold out hope. Remember the story of the prodigal son? Jesus told this parable, found in Luke 15:11–32, to remind us never to give up on those who stray. After demanding and then losing his inheritance, the younger son in the parable returned home to ask forgiveness for his many indiscretions. Rather than reprimand his son or tell him, "It's about time you came crawling back," the father rejoiced and embraced his lost son, throwing a great banquet in his honor.

Where did this attitude come from? It came from a heart of love and compassion, from someone who never gave up on his son. If you need an example of someone who has this heart, you need only think of your heavenly Father, who has never stopped loving you and has never given up on you.

"I have loved you, my people, with an everlasting love.
With unfailing love I have drawn you to myself."

JEREMIAH 31:3

- God will never refuse someone who wants to come back.

- Children bring us happiness and children bring us grief. Either way, they bring us tears.

- Hope doesn't come from what *you* can do. Hope comes from what *God* can do.

- When we believe that God won't give us more than we can bear, we can bear much more than we thought possible.

- Knowing that God won't give up on you keeps you from giving up on others.

Marriage isn't a battle that
someone is supposed to win.

Anonymous

THIRTEEN

WHEN A MARRIAGE GOES BAD

Abraham Lincoln once said: "Marriage is neither heaven nor hell. It is simply purgatory." Many people would agree with that statement, but an engaged couple might express an opposing viewpoint. No one enters into marriage with the expectation that their lives together will be mediocre. They aren't expecting a tolerable coexistence. Rather, they enter matrimony with the anticipation that a lifetime of wedded "bliss" awaits them.

No marriage is ideal or easy. Perhaps Adam and Eve came the closest. (He didn't have to hear about all of the other men she could have married—and she didn't have to hear about how his mother cooked better.) But even their blissful moments of marriage in the Garden of Eden were cut short by the intrusion of sin.

We live in a fallen world where the infection of sin affects all of us, individually and as married couples. The ideal marriage that was hoped for on the wedding day can't be found after the honeymoon. Why? Because neither the husband nor the wife is ideal to begin with. Each one is flawed, with his or her own idiosyncrasies. Immature neurotic traits do not evaporate when the wedding ring is slipped on the finger; they are actually magnified by the immature neurotic behaviors of the other spouse.

When a marriage begins to disintegrate, there is friction between the spouses. That dislocation of the relationship is always difficult to endure, but both individuals know that it will happen. The often unexpected and unarticulated pain of marriage difficulties comes from a sense of disillusionment. At some point, each spouse will come to the shocking realization that their romantic dreams of matrimonial bliss are totally unrealistic. The wife is dejected because she had envisioned a continued courtship with lasting, loving attention from the man she married; this is now just a dashed dream. The husband is disconsolate because he has not received the love and respect he had assumed would always be forthcoming from his bride; the stark reality of it all hurts.

Where is God in all of this? Can He be found? Or are those who suffer from a broken marriage relegated to the position of second-class citizens in God's eyes? It is bad enough that they must endure the whispers, gossip, and condescension of others; must they now bear God's disdain as well? The answer is a resounding "No!"

Whether a marriage is irrevocably broken or still hanging together by a thread, it is important to realize that a person's needs will never be completely fulfilled by a spouse. That is an unreasonable—and impossible—expectation. While a loving spouse can be supportive in many ways, only God can provide you with a sense of worth and wholeness. Don't expect a spouse to provide what is available only from God. This means that all is not lost for the husband and wife after the marriage has terminated. God is still there, even if the spouse is not.

For those struggling marriages that still have a chance, the focus of each spouse needs to be outwardly directed. Instead of seeking personal fulfillment, the primary goal should be the fulfillment of the other spouse's needs. Of course, this won't be easy if the other spouse is uncooperative and not interested in reciprocating. But here again, God is the solution. He can provide the strength to show love to someone who is acting in an unloving manner.

It is often heard in a wedding ceremony that a successful

marriage is not a union of two people but rather a union of three: a man, a woman, and God. That is true. But it is equally true that God needs to be viewed as an essential component in your life when the marriage is unsuccessful.

- God doesn't love you less just because you've been unsuccessful in love.

- God should be the love of your life.

- A good marriage won't happen unless you get a divorce from yourself. You can't love God or your spouse if you love yourself more.

- Marriage is the most intimate and difficult of relationships. Although God intends it for a lifetime, life goes on after a marriage stops.

- Don't be desperate to get married. Be desperate for God.

Children begin by loving their parents;
as they grow older, they judge them;
sometimes they forgive them.

Oscar Wilde

FOURTEEN

When Parents Attack

When it comes to the hard stuff in our families, it seems as though our spouses and/or our children are usually at the center of controversy. But there are times when our parents can be difficult—or downright impossible. Even worse, parents can sometimes cause extraordinary distress in our own lives.

The most blatant problem is outright abuse, when a parent inflicts harm on a child. Sadly, alcohol often plays a role in such deplorable behavior. Other times darker forces can be at work. Some parents wouldn't think of physically harming their children, but they see nothing wrong with berating them verbally. A parent may even think he is building "character" into a child by constantly criticizing and belittling, as if that will build a defense against the criticism a child is likely to face in the "real world."

And then there are those parents who deliberately withhold their affection and support from one or more of their children—or they may "play favorites," which has nearly the same effect. This may be the most subtle and insidious behavior of all. With overt physical or verbal abuse, as awful as that is, at least a child knows where he stands. When people get the "silent treatment," though, it's hard to know what to do because they don't know what's really going on.

Thankfully, some of these destructive parental behaviors disappear when children become adults. But others remain well into adulthood. Perhaps you are dealing with a parent who criticizes or ignores or even attacks you. It may be in your parent's nature to treat you this way. What can you do? Should you ignore it and allow the extreme criticism to negatively impact the way you relate to your mother or father, or should you once and for all confront the situation head-on—no matter what the consequences?

We would suggest that you neither ignore it nor confront it. What may work best is to honor your father and your mother. Sound strange? Absolutely. To honor someone who abuses you runs contrary to logic—not to mention all that is in you. Yet that's exactly what the Bible tells us to do. In fact, it's one of the Ten Commandments, and the first one that comes with a promise:

> *And this is the promise: If you honor your father and mother, "you will live a long life, full of blessing."*
>
> EPHESIANS 6:3

Do you see what's going on here? *Honoring your parents brings positive benefits to you.* Does this mean you say some nice things about your strange and possibly abusive parents just so you can live a life full of blessing? Well, that's not a bad trade-off, is it? Besides, there must be more to this little deal God established than meets the eye. Indeed there is.

If honoring your parents brings blessing, then perhaps it follows that dishonoring them brings problems. Think of your own life for a moment. If you are harboring ill feelings or bitterness toward one or both of your parents, how is it going with you? Is your resentment having some negative effect on your parents, or are *you* the one suffering?

Is it possible that God wants us to honor the people who brought us into the world—despite their faults—so that we might be better people ourselves? Beyond that, is it possible that an irregular parent might just live up to our sincere attempts to honor him or her? Not only is it possible, it is also likely. When you withhold honor from your parents, no matter how justified you feel in doing so, you are withholding God's promise and the blessing that goes with it. But when you honor them, you open the door to His blessings.

- Family abuse can be cyclical, but it doesn't have to be perpetual.

- Playing favorites does no one any good—not even the one being favored.

- The person most affected by a bitter attitude is the one with the attitude.

- Honoring people doesn't mean you always agree with them, but it does mean you always respect them.

- God never breaks a promise. Never.

How many days have you cried for me?

How many tears have you dried for me?

How many days have you worried long?

How many years have you filled with song?

How many times have I hurt your heart?

How many times have we had to part?

How many prayers have you said for me?

How many miles have you walked for me?

Nobody knows but you, Mother.

Anonymous

FIFTEEN

A Mother's Anguish

He tips the scale at about three hundred pounds. He might be missing a front tooth. His hands are bloody from the field of battle. His uniform is grass-stained from scrimmages earlier in the game. Every muscle in his body aches from the brutal punishment he has inflicted on the opposing football team. But as the television camera catches him sitting on the bench, his spirit is lifted and he flashes a broad grin before exaggerating the enunciation of: "Hi, Mom!" It is a scene that is commonplace in our culture. But the parental preference is curious. How come a "Hi, Dad" is never uttered?

Without doubt, there is a special bond between a mother

and her child. And we aren't just referring to the umbilical cord connection. The instincts and character of motherhood transcend the womb experience and the journey down the birth canal. *Having* a child doesn't make a woman a mother any more than owning a piano makes a person a musician. Oh, certainly the process begins at conception, but the status of *motherhood* is conferred in the progression of life from infancy to childhood, to adolescence, to adulthood:

- Motherhood involves the apprehension of caring for a newborn that was delivered without an owner's instruction manual.
- Motherhood is earned in the state of exhaustion caused by monitoring the constant movements that progress from carpet crawler to curtain climber.
- Motherhood involves multitasking among the roles of chauffeur, nurse, cheerleader, disciplinarian, counselor, friend, cook, maid, and craft supervisor.
- Motherhood witnesses the simple joys of childhood and the angst of adolescence.

- Motherhood suffers the growing pains of the teenage years, with the hope of being rewarded with close friendship when maturity kicks in.
- Motherhood is a 24/7 job that starts at birth and never stops.

The joys of motherhood are some of life's sweetest rewards. But the anguish of motherhood is some of life's hardest stuff. While the anguish of some mothers is intensified by tragedy, all mothers experience the pain of "letting go." This is an almost constant pain, especially for those mothers who cherish every stage in their child's development. A mother experiences the anguish of "letting go" when

- infancy ends with the transition from the crib to the "big kid's bed";
- her child starts school;
- her child would rather play with friends than hang out with Mom;
- the teenage years begin a search for independence with an accompanying "silent treatment";

- the bedroom is emptied as the child moves out of the house;
- a wedding means that the child's primary confidant will be a spouse rather than Mom;
- the role of grandparent keeps you involved but clearly on the sidelines of the family.

This continual process of a mother "letting go" can result in a lifetime of prolonged anguish. There is always a foreboding element of the unknown that accompanies letting go. But the fear and apprehension can be dispelled if the mother knows who she is letting go to. If the mother lives her life in a vacuum without any spiritual connections, then she loses every time she lets go. She can't get back what she must give up; she is forced to forfeit something that she used to hold dear. But if she lets go of these things to God—realizing that He is in control of the circumstances of her child's life—then letting go means that things are *better* because they are within God's plan.

For every mother, there is a big difference between "letting go" and "letting God." A mother's concern for her child can turn from anxiety to anticipation. The difference is determined by the mother's spiritual perspective. "Letting go" is a very good thing if you are entrusting your child to God's care and direction.

. . .IN THE HARD STUFF

* Don't hold on to your children so tightly that God can't move them.

* As your children get older, the best mothering involves less smothering.

* It is a mother's job to raise her children to be independent and self-sufficient. She is to be praised when that happens (although she will later regret that she was so good at it).

* "Letting go" is difficult for a mother—but if it doesn't happen, it is disastrous for the child.

* Some of the greatest joys of motherhood can only be experienced from a distance.

T here must always be a struggle
between a father and son,
while one aims at power
and the other at independence.

Samuel Johnson

SIXTEEN

A FATHER'S GRIEF

There is a story in the Old Testament about David, Israel's greatest monarch. David is one of the most recognizable figures in history. Nearly everybody has heard about David defeating the unbeatable Goliath with one swoosh of his slingshot. We know about David's friendship with Jonathan and his conflict with Jonathan's father, King Saul. And who hasn't read about David's great sin with Bathsheba and the murder of her husband, a loyal soldier named Uriah?

David was a complex man—a great poet, a mighty warrior, a conquering king—whose amazing virtues were sometimes over-shadowed by his considerable vices. He loved God deeply, and God considered David a man after His own heart. But that didn't stop David from experiencing great grief, and none more agonizing that the two times he lost a child.

If you are a father, and you are grieving the loss of a child—whether that child has physically left this world or is emotionally detached from you—there is much you can learn from David's biblical example. The way he dealt with the massive grief in his life may help you with something you are now experiencing, or prepare you for something to come.

The first son David lost was the baby he had with Bathsheba. The baby became deathly ill shortly after birth, sending David into great anguish. The king, going for days without food, pleaded with God to spare his child. When the baby died, David's advisors were reluctant to tell their king, fearing he might go into a depression from which he would not recover. But that isn't how David grieved. When he learned of the baby's death, David pulled himself together and went to the Temple, where he worshiped God. His advisors were amazed and more than a little puzzled. Why the change?

"We don't understand you," they told him. "While the baby was still living, you wept and refused to eat. But now that the baby is dead, you have stopped mourning and are eating again."

2 Samuel 12:21

While his baby was alive, David fasted and prayed that God would be gracious to him and allow his baby to live. But when his baby died, David realized that God's grace was just as real. It is at this point that David gave comfort to all who have ever lost a child. David said, "I will go to him one day, but he cannot return to me" (2 Samuel 12:23), thereby giving us hope that our little ones who depart this world immediately go into God's presence.

David lost another child under dramatically different circumstances. His adult son Absalom could have been the poster child for rebellion. He opposed his father at every turn, finally challenging the throne by amassing an army against David, who was forced to flee the capital city of Jerusalem. Absalom engaged his father in battle and was cut down by those loyal to the king. Rather than rejoice in his rebellious son's defeat, David lamented his loss.

"O my son Absalom! My son, my son Absalom! If only I could have died instead of you! O Absalom, my son, my son."

2 SAMUEL 18:33

David never stopped loving his child, even in Absalom's deepest rebellion—and neither should you. A parent's love should never falter, just as our own Father's love for us never wanes.

- The reason we can learn from characters in scripture is because the Bible tells the truth about people, warts and all.

- A father who isn't emotionally attached to his children isn't much of a father.

- If you believe in your children, they will believe in themselves.

- God has children but no grandchildren— because each of us must come to Him directly.

Growing old is like being
increasingly penalized for a crime
you haven't committed.

Anthony Powell

SEVENTEEN

CARING FOR AGING PARENTS

Sociologists have a term for them: the "Hinge Generation." These are the adults who simultaneously have responsibility for their minor children and for their aged parents. It's a relatively new generational demographic that occurs because married couples are having children at a later age and advances in health care allow people to live longer. Instead of an average life expectancy in the upper sixties, it is now more common for people to live into their seventies, eighties, and even nineties.

While the increase in life expectancy is a wonderful thing, it is accompanied by challenges to traditional family dynamics. There are unspoken—and often misunderstood—tensions that develop. The logistics of caring for an aging parent often create mounting frustrations for each generation. Both feel imposed upon.

It is easy for children to harbor resentment for the care they are required to render to their parents. They quite understandably feel:

- *A loss of freedom.* They already have a hectic schedule and a calendar full of commitments: taking care of their children, managing a home, pressures on the job, and social obligations. What little free time they once had must now be allocated to caring for a parent. While they might never refer to it as a "burden," it is certainly an obligation that is disruptive to their family life and previous routine.

- *A loss of context.* These adult children suffer a loss that relates to their station in life. Up until this point, they have always been able to seek wisdom and comfort from their parents. But they are now deprived of parental guidance due perhaps to Alzheimer's disease or the introspection and self-centeredness that often accompanies old age. Although they have a parent who is still living, they have no one who assumes the parental role in their lives. The declining capacities of the parents have effectively left these children as orphans. They must mourn the loss of a parental figure in their lives while still attending to the needs of their parents.

But these children must also realize that their parents have undergone some drastic changes in their circumstances, too; many times it is not a change of their choosing, being forced upon them by declining health. Their physical limitations and diminishing mental acuity can result in a significant restriction of the activities they previously enjoyed. Despite the efforts of their adult children to provide appropriate living arrangements, the older generation feels:

- *A loss of independence.* Their lives are suddenly defined more by the things they *can't* do than by the things that they are *able* to do. They may be told when to eat and what to eat. They may have lost their mobility, either by being deprived of driving privileges or by being confined to a wheelchair or forced to use a walker. They may not even be allowed to handle their own finances.
- *A loss of dignity.* They are well aware of the fact that

their loss of freedom places them in a circumstance somewhat similar to a small child. Their own children are now their care providers—in a classic role reversal, the parent has become the child. While this is a part of a natural progression, it is nonetheless humiliating. These once proud and independent people are now living under stringent rules and regulations that clearly imply they can't be trusted to make decisions for themselves.

This sociological phenomenon has not caught God off guard. The advances in medical science that contributed to these circumstances do not surprise Him. He is not powerless to bring strength and love into these difficult situations.

Remember that God is the grand designer of the family. The family unit is so sacred that He uses it to describe His relationship with us. (He is our heavenly Father and we are His children.) Before the creation of the universe He knew that the twenty-first century would find adult children caring for their parents. This is a circumstance that is clearly within His plan, so He will certainly make His spiritual strength available to those who are in it.

- God honors the love that is shown among family members.

- Imagine how humbling it must be for a parent to be dependent upon a child for care. What a privilege it is for a child to reciprocate to his or her parent in this fashion.

- Care for your aged parents with the same love and mercy God has shown to you.

- Faults of parents should not be revisited upon them by their children.

- Take good care of your parents in their old age. Remember that your children are watching you.

- Treat your parents in their old age in the manner that you hope to be treated by your own children.

We will never forget them,
nor the last time we saw them. . .
as they prepared for their long journey
and waved good-bye and slipped
the surly bonds of Earth
to touch the face of God.

Ronald Reagan

EIGHTEEN

THE LONG GOOD-BYE

Like a black cloud hovering on the horizon, the specter of Alzheimer's disease looms. Already five million people in the United States and thirty million worldwide are afflicted with dementia in its most common forms—Alzheimer's disease and vascular dementia—impacting the lives of tens of millions more in the immediate circles of family and friends.

Those numbers are expected to grow dramatically as our population ages. About one in ten people over sixty-five, and as many as half of all people over the age of eight-five, have Alzheimer's. It is now the eighth leading cause of death for people aged sixty-five and older. Health care costs are estimated to be more than fifty billion dollars per year.

It's not just the costly and deadly nature of this insidious condition that is most troubling. The personal impact of dementia and Alzheimer's, which Nancy Reagan called "the long good-bye," exacts the greatest toll. This is an illness that makes it hard for people to remember, think, and speak. It can make them seem moody or act strangely. The strong and vibrant man or woman you once knew as a husband or wife, mom or dad, grandfather or grandmother, uncle, aunt, or friend changes in ways that are subtle at first and then dramatic. On the outside they look normal, but on the inside things are clearly different. There seems to be an emptiness, a loss of personal identity. Dementia is the slow death of the brain, and as yet the cause cannot be entirely explained. Nor is there an entirely effective treatment or a cure.

But there is hope! Dr. Walt Russell, New Testament professor at Talbot School of Theology and a good friend, knows that now. Seventeen years ago he came face-to-face with the reality of dementia in his own mother. For seventeen years he watched her slide "more and more deeply into its abyss." For Walt, dementia isn't just a faceless statistic. It has his mother's face.

Just before his mother died, Walt felt compelled to write her a letter, reflecting on her life and the way he had been dealing with her condition. The letter led Walt to wrestle with some of the hard questions surrounding dementia. Because Walt's mother was a long-time Christian, many of these questions took on a spiritual nature:

- What became of her relationship with God when she lost most of her ability to think and reason?
- Did she continue to enjoy God's loving care and the presence of the Holy Spirit?
- Did God continue to care for her, Spirit-to-spirit, in spite of those damaged brain cells?
- Did she experience, in the depths of her soul, the promise of Jesus never to leave or forsake her?
- Did her soul still have the capacity to will—to choose to trust God—in spite of her dementia?

As Walt wrestled with these questions and the larger issues surrounding them, he came to a place where he believed his mother would have answered "yes" to all his questions. "My sense is that *her inability* to express an awareness of God's tender presence with her had no effect on *His ability* to be with her in the struggle. My hope and prayer is that she was never really alone in her dementia all those years."[1]

If you are struggling with a family member or friend with dementia, may this be your hope. And may you offer this hope to others caught up in the struggle.

> *That is why we never give up. Though our bodies are dying, our spirits are being renewed every day.*
>
> 2 CORINTHIANS 4:16

- Even though a person cannot think, it doesn't mean he or she cannot feel.

- It's comforting to know that God continues to love us even when we can't love Him back.

- The measure of a culture is in how it treats the weak and infirm.

- The value of life should never be determined by the quality of life.

- When Jesus said He would never leave us nor forsake us, He meant it.

God expects but one thing of you,

and that is that you. . .

let God be God in you.

Meister Eckhart

NINETEEN

HONORING GOD

God came up with the idea of families. If He created the concept, then you know it must be a good one. But any observer of the modern-day family would quickly conclude that the design isn't working—there are too many dysfunctional families. Has the concept become outmoded due to cultural advances or adversities? Is it now a cruel practical joke that God plays on humanity by insisting that people artificially hang together—even when they are repulsed by each other?

The problem of the dysfunctional family is not the fault of God, nor is it a defect in His design. The problem is that individual family members have not been operating according to God's principles. His intent is that we function in the family for the sake of the other members:

- The husband is to love his wife.
- The wife is to respect her husband.
- The parents are to care for their children.
- The children are to honor their parents.

Well, it looks good on paper—but why doesn't it work in our living rooms? Because we selfishly twist God's principles for family life. For many people, their family mantra has become "All for one, and I'm the one." And the self-centeredness of only one member in a family is enough to make the entire group dysfunctional. So the breakdown can be caused by:

- an overbearing parent;
- a rebellious teenager;
- a disobedient child;
- an unfaithful spouse;
- a non-confrontive or enabling spouse;

- an intrusive in-law;
- an envious sibling.

Even if all of the members of a family are well-intentioned, the breakdown of relationships can be initiated by outside factors such as financial problems, health challenges, or conflicts at work. The stress caused by intervening events can cause family members to respond in less-than-loving ways to each other. And that is putting it mildly.

What role can you play when the disintegration of a family seems irreversible? How can you alone attempt to change the direction once the downward spiral of familial dysfunction has begun? Is it realistic to think that a broken family can be restored if only one person is committed to pursuing reconciliation?

The solution to these problems begins with a simple rule: Honor God. That is what He expects of you. That and that alone. By honoring God in everything you do and say, you'll be a positive influence in your family. You aren't responsible for—or capable of— changing the attitudes of the other members of your family. The best thing you can do for your family is to infuse it with the influence of godly character. That *can* come from you.

Will this be difficult? You bet! But notice that God's principles for family living are not conditioned on the reciprocal behavior of the others. In other words:

- the husband is to love his wife, even if she is ill-tempered;
- the wife is to respect her husband, even if he is lazy and inattentive;
- the parents are to care for their children, even if they are unappreciative and disobedient; and
- the children are to honor their parents, even if they are unfair and restrictive.

So that is your challenge. And that is your solution. Love when you don't feel like it. Love when you aren't loved back. Love when it appears that there is no hope of reconciliation. You will be honoring God by honoring His design for the operation of the family. That is the best thing you can do for your family. It is the best thing you can do for yourself.

- Every unhappy family is unhappy in its own unique way. Happy families are all happy in the same way—they are implementing God's principles.

- God wants to have an influence in your family. You are the way He intends to accomplish that.

- You have control over your actions and attitudes. Trust the results to God.

- The greatest test of love is whether we can love those who act unlovingly towards us.

- We honor God when we commit ourselves to our family. We dishonor God if we give up on our family.

Creditors have
better memories than debtors.

Benjamin Franklin

TWENTY

IN OVER YOUR HEAD

Financial problems can crop up by themselves if you aren't careful, but this situation can usually be fixed with a sensible fiscal fitness program (i.e., a budget). There are financial problems of a more severe variety, however, and they usually have a precipitating cause. You've heard it said that "every storm cloud has a silver lining." That may be true some of the time, but there is always something that financial storm clouds have in common: a big price tag.

It is bad enough when you are forced to endure hard times, but the burden is even heavier when there's a financial cost that wasn't in the budget:

- Having a prolonged illness is bad enough, but in addition to the suffering, you miss a few weeks' work and go without the paycheck you need for the medical bills (and the other "luxuries" of life like rent, food, and utilities).
- Being in a car wreck leaves you sore and without transportation, but on top of that you're stuck with repair bills (or at least your insurance deductible) to pay.

And so it goes with almost all of life's tragedies. Whenever there is a challenge in your life, there is often an accompanying adverse financial effect that makes matters worse. Think about the additional costs associated with:

- a disabled child;
- divorce;
- death of a loved one.

Many times, the pressure of financial commitments can overshadow the precipitating cause. And while time may provide a remedy to the underlying problem (you recover from surgery, the grief over a death may subside, or you get hired for a new job), it may seem that you will never be able to pull out of the downward financial spiral that has begun.

At the most basic level, the solution to financial problems is just a matter of knowing your directions:

> If your *out*go exceeds your *in*come,
> then your *up*keep will be your *down*fall.

So the solution to any financial problem is simple—spend less than you make. But this maxim of money management rings hollow if you:

- lack any present source of income;
- have already reduced your lifestyle to basic necessities;
- can't downsize your living expenses fast enough to stay in proportion to your shrinking income; or
- have responsibility for the "upkeep" of others who, because of health or age, have no ability to contribute to financial production.

Let's face it. Once that income/expense ratio gets out of whack, your bank balance isn't the only thing headed downward. . . so is your outlook.

It may be difficult to stay God-focused when the creditors are calling every night. But you need to maintain a spiritual perspective. That growing stack of unpaid bills is intimidating—and depressing—so consider what benefit and hope can be found in your present situation:

- *God has promised to provide all our needs.* Philippians 4:19 says, "And this same God who takes care of me will supply all your needs from his glorious riches, which have been given to us in Christ Jesus." Of course, it might be appropriate to clarify the distinction between what is a *need* and what is a *luxury.* But you can rely on God's promises to get the *needs* covered.

- *Financial problems teach us to depend on God as the source of everything.* Financial difficulties are a humbling experience, but such circumstances force us to realize that we are not the masters of our own economic destiny.

- *A prolonged cash flow crisis should make us much more sympathetic to those who have no hope of escaping a life of abject poverty.* Ranging from the homeless in your city to citizens of many third-world countries, there are millions of people who would be envious of your economic status. No matter how difficult it is for you, you have it better than many in America and most others around the globe. Maybe your experience will make you more sympathetic to their plight. . .and more willing to give financial assistance to them when you are able to do so. The Bible even has a promise for those who give to the less fortunate: "Those who refresh others will themselves be refreshed" (Proverbs 11:25).

It is not likely that God will solve your economic plight with a set of winning lottery numbers. So don't expect a quick fix to your money problems. But don't rely on yourself for the entire solution, either. Work hard at money management, but include God in the process. He didn't get you into the problem, but He can help get you out of it.

- Money management should be considered a spiritual matter.

- Don't expect God to bail you out if you haven't included Him in your decisions.

- When you've dug yourself into a pit of debt, there's only one direction you can look: up.

- The only debt you can never repay is God's love for you. Work on paying all of the others with His help.

- God may not plan for you to be rich, but He certainly doesn't want you to be in debt.

There is only one class in the community
that thinks more about money than the rich,
and that is the poor.
The poor can think of nothing else.
That is the misery of being poor.

Oscar Wilde

TWENTY-ONE

FROM BUSTED TO BELIEF

There are times when you realize that, while life is hard, it could get worse. That can be a sobering prospect, but you might find comfort in the fact that you aren't as low as you could be:

- Illness is bad, but at least you aren't dead.
- Being underemployed is bad, but being unemployed would be worse.
- Loneliness is bad, but at least you're not hated by everyone you know.
- Being in debt is bad, but you're not in a debtor's prison.

Actually, debtor's prisons were closed more than one hundred years ago. So now when you hit bottom financially, bankruptcy is as bad as it gets. But that's bad—you can't get any lower. Unlike being in debt (which can keep accumulating), bankruptcy is the financial equivalent of waving the white flag. You give up. You concede. You are defeated. You're basically saying, "Come and take everything I've got."

In most respects, total financial failure is a bad place to be. But from a spiritual perspective, it's also a place where you can begin to deepen your relationship with God. Perhaps God considers it necessary to bring you to a place of complete financial brokenness so you can understand that *God is all I've got.*

When you've had everything taken from you, one thing is painfully obvious: All you have is God. When your cars are repossessed, you still have God. When the bank has foreclosed on your home, you still have God. When your savings are depleted and the cupboards are bare, you still have God. When you have lost all your worldly possessions, you still have God. He will never leave you or forget you. He is your one and only constant in life. Let the fact of His eternal presence be a comfort to you. You are never without anything because you always have God.

But understanding that God is all you have is just the first step. As you deepen your relationship with God, you can discover that *God is all I need*.

Living at the lowest rung of the financial ladder can teach you that so much of our material world is superfluous. At the most elementary level, very few things are necessities of life. Because God has promised to provide everything we *need*, He is all we need. He'll make sure we have the basics (although He is likely to expect we'll be contributing effort and energy). Once the basics are covered, we can truly enjoy the non-material blessings that God offers (love, joy, peace, etc.).

But it doesn't stop at that point. There is one further step in the process of maturing in your faith. Once you understand that God is the source of everything you need, the material objects of life become distractions. Recognizing that God is the sole source of everything that really matters, you may suddenly come to the liberating realization that *God is all I want*.

Now you've reached the depth of spiritual maturity that God desires for you. When you aren't worried about what you *have*, and when you aren't distracted by what you *need*, you are free from the entanglements that accompany financial worries. You realize that material possessions have absolutely no significance when compared to the privilege of having a personal acquaintanceship with God. If the things that money can buy divert your attention from God, then you don't want them. Whether you have wealth or not becomes irrelevant so long as you can have God.

Is this last stage of spiritual maturity unrealistic? Is it purely theoretical and impossible to reach? It may seem so, but that is only because we have not broken free from the grip of materialism. For the apostle Paul—who had experienced both a life of privilege and a life of poverty—his financial status was irrelevant:

> *I have learned how to get along happily whether I have much or little. I know how to live on almost nothing or with everything. I have learned the secret of living in every situation, whether it is with a full stomach or empty, with plenty or little.*
>
> PHILIPPIANS 4:11–12

What was Paul's secret? Realizing that God was all he had, all he needed, and all he wanted. Make that secret yours.

- You'll enjoy life more if you value the quality of relationships more than the quantity of possessions.

- Maybe it takes having nothing to discover how little you really need.

- Going without can be a good thing if it causes you to go with God.

- Sometimes you have to look past the possessions to discover God's presence.

- No matter how little you have, you're never broke if you have God. No matter how rich you are, you're living in poverty without Him.

T housands upon thousands
are yearly brought into a state of real poverty
by their great anxiety not to be thought poor.

William Cobbett

TWENTY-TWO

WHAT WILL OTHERS THINK?

When the tragedies in your life are the result of factors beyond your control, you will be showered with sympathy from others. Consolation and compassion will be extended to you if:

- You are diagnosed with brain cancer;
- A close member of your family dies;
- A drunk driver hits your car from behind and leaves you with spinal cord injuries; or
- You lose your job due to downsizing by the company.

Despite the difficulties you are enduring, you will feel loved and supported by the people you know.

It is quite a different situation, however, if the hard circumstances in your life are the direct result of dumb decisions you made. No one is going to feel sorry for you if:

- You can't make your mortgage payment because you sold your Kia Sportage and financed a Hummer;
- You quit your job at the architectural firm because you believed a spam e-mail that said you could make five thousand dollars a month in your spare time addressing envelopes;
- You sell all your furniture at a yard sale to buy lottery tickets because you had a premonition that the winning Super Lotto numbers would match your child's Social Security Number; or
- You develop a severe gastrointestinal disorder caused by your attempts to get listed in *The Guinness Book of World Records* for consumption of Krispy Kreme doughnuts.

In such cases, you may be ridiculed unmercifully—and you will have deserved it. But this is a good thing because the fear of what other people will think about you probably restrains you from doing foolish things that might otherwise be tempting.

> *The wise inherit honor, but fools are put to shame!*
>
> PROVERBS 3:35

Let's face it. Much of our lives is governed by what other people might think. Sometimes it motivates us to push harder because we enjoy the accolades. Other times, our fear of the opinion of others can be debilitating. When we are going through tough times that we have caused, our fear of what others think can make life worse than the difficulties we are in:

- We might think doing nothing is better than admitting our stupidity.
- We become reclusive because we want to hide from the people who might be mocking us.
- We don't ask for help or advice because we

want to keep our problems as confidential as
possible.

- We don't take the appropriate corrective action
  because it might bring more publicity to our
  embarrassment.

If you are going through some hard stuff, and if you are
crippled by fear of the negative opinions of others, there are a few
important things you need to remember:

1. *Other people aren't focused on your situation as
   much as you think they are.* Your family and
   friends may care about you, but they've got
   other things in their lives that take higher
   priority. They are too busy thinking about
   themselves to be worrying about you. In fact,
   they may not even be aware of *your* problems
   because they are too preoccupied worrying
   what *you* might think about *their* personal
   humiliations.

2. *God is the only one who is thinking about you all of*

the time. Though we all tend to be self-centered, God thinks about each of us even more than we think about ourselves. He is thinking about you all the time. If He has a desk, there's probably a framed 5 x 7 picture of you on it. (We jest, but you get the point.) Because of His concern for you, God knows exactly what is going on in your life. Don't waste mental energy wondering if you can hide your plight from God. He knows the mess you're in—but that's a good thing. (See the next point.)

3. *God won't snicker at your problems; He is only interested in helping you.* How fortunate for you that God not only knows all about your problems, He also wants to help you get out of them. And, unlike most of your friends and family, He has the ability to help you (which is one of the benefits of God's omnipotence).

Stop worrying about what others think of your problems. That's only counterproductive. Instead, remember that God is on your side. In the final analysis, that is where you are going to find ultimate comfort and resolution.

> *I trust in God, so why should I be afraid? What can mere mortals do to me?* PSALM 56:11

* Your friends may never let you live down a mistake. But God is quick to forgive and forget when you ask Him.

* Worry about what God thinks. The opinions of other people have no eternal consequences.

* You can't effectively deal with your problems if you are paralyzed by fear of what others will think.

* The time when the opinion of others is most useful is when it prevents you from doing something foolish.

* You can't hide from God what He already knows about. You might as well ask His help to deal with it.

W ork is an extension of personality.

It is achievement.

It is one of the ways in which a person defines himself,

measures his worth and his humanity.

Peter F. Drucker

TWENTY-THREE

A LOSS OF SELF

Sometimes events and circumstances—such as illness, financial struggles, or broken relationships—are the "hard stuff" of life. But sometimes the tough stuff is simply a matter of unfulfilled expectations. This occurs when your life isn't really bad, but something less than you wanted it to be. In comparison to your friends, your circumstance may not be difficult—but it can be very depressing stacked up against what you have been desperately hoping for.

Your unmet expectations can take many forms:

- You lost your job.
- You didn't get promoted.

- You've been demoted.
- You haven't attained the financial security you expected.
- You're in a dead-end job you hate.
- You never obtained that educational degree.

Disappointments, if not dealt with, can gnaw away at you. The disappointment over unmet expectations evolves into disappointment with yourself. There is an insidious shift in your unhappiness. It moves from dejection over *what* you have failed to achieve and turns into a disappointment over *who* you are:

- I lost my job, so I'm an incompetent person.
- I never completed any degree, so I lack ambition.
- I didn't get the promotion, so I'm a loser.
- I'm financially insecure, so I'm a big failure.

Don't fall into the trap of defining yourself by what you have accomplished—or failed to. Your sense of self should be determined by your character traits (integrity, friendliness, loyalty, responsibility, etc.), not by the achievements on your résumé.

In case you doubt a change of perspective will ease the pain of an unmet expectation, take the "Eulogy Quiz." Don't worry; there is only one question:

> When the eulogy is given at your funeral, would you rather have your life evaluated by
>> A. the status of your achievements; or
>> B. the lives that were positively impacted by your character?

Few people would choose option A. Achievements quickly become empty and meaningless when you have been placed six feet below the earth's surface. On the other hand, kindness and encouragement to others (option B) make a legacy that remains long after your death.

And remember this: You aren't the best judge of the significance of your unmet expectations. You're not objective. After all, you're likely to be tempted to attribute too much importance to the thing you have been hoping for. (People most often obsess over expectations that will make their lives easier or make them appear successful to others—things related to prestige, status, or wealth. People very seldom evaluate themselves according to the more substantive and internal character qualities of life—things that aren't as readily apparent to others.)

Why not turn the matter of your unmet expectations over to God? If God thinks it is essential that you obtain what you have hoped for, He can work in the circumstances of your life to bring it about. But don't expect God to lose sleep over the job you lost or some other opportunity that passed you by. Of course those things are important to Him (because they are important to you), but He is less concerned about your status and more concerned about the kind of person you are.

In God's paradigm, you are not evaluated by what you have failed to achieve. He is more interested in the character you display in the face of your unmet expectations.

- Are you going to mope or are you going to become motivated?
- Are you going to be critically introspective, or will you look expectantly for what God has next?
- Are you going to spiral downward from disappointment to despair, or will you display the character of overcoming your failure?

God is the best career advisor you can find. Include Him in the evaluation process of determining what you should do and who you should become.

. . .In the Hard Stuff

- The kind of person you are is a matter of your character, not your circumstances.

- Don't let a missed opportunity be the cause of missing God's presence in your life.

- An unmet expectation is the perfect occasion for meeting God.

- God cares more about your character than your résumé.

- When people are fondly remembered, it is for the compassion in their hearts—not for the list of their accomplishments.

God has given us two hands—
one for receiving and the other for giving.

Billy Graham

TWENTY-FOUR

GIVING TO GOD

W herever your treasure is, there your heart and thoughts will also be." In that simple sentence, Jesus touched the center point of human nature when it comes to money and possessions. If we are storing up treasure in heaven, our hearts will follow after God and His eternal values. If our goal is to store up treasure on earth, our hearts will more often than not be bound by greed and insecurity, caught in the tension between always wanting more and never having enough.

Is your life characterized by one frustrating financial crisis after another? Is your mind preoccupied with money woes? Do you wish you could give to more worthy causes, but never seem to have enough left over at the end of the month? Then it's likely that you are attempting to store up your treasure on earth.

If that's the case, you aren't a bad person—and you certainly aren't alone. Many people who desire to follow God with all their heart struggle in this area. In fact, all believers—if they are being honest—have to fight the urge to build up earthly treasure. We are so concerned about making and protecting our money that we have a natural tendency to take our focus off heaven, where all we have comes from in the first place.

We may think we earn money and own things, but the reality is that everything we have comes from God. We aren't owners; we are stewards, entrusted by God to wisely manage the resources He has given us. Everything we have—money, possessions, even our abilities and talents—are gifts from God. Of course, God wants us to enjoy what He has given us, but He also wants us to acknowledge His ownership by giving it back to Him. In fact, God promises to bless us if we do! By contrast, He will withhold His blessing if we don't.

So how do we give back to God? We can't suddenly give Him money we don't have. It starts small, with little amounts of our money and time, given to God with open hands. And it takes thought and prayer. You need to carefully consider what God wants you to do. In time, God will show you some specific opportunities, and you will build up your ability to give to God. Then, as you do, your heart will be blessed, and you will find yourself wanting to give more. That's just the way it works.

If you are wondering where you should begin giving to God, you can start by giving generously to others. An altruistic and willing heart pleases God because it takes your eyes off yourself and puts them on the people around you. "For God loves the person who gives cheerfully" (2 Corinthians 9:7).

Here's something else about giving to God. When you give generously and cheerfully to others—whether it's to your church, a charitable organization, or individuals serving Christ in ministry—you don't have to worry about your own needs, because God will be generous to you. "Then you will always have everything you need and plenty left over to share with others" (2 Corinthians 9:8).

Another principle to follow in your giving is to help the poor. As the scriptures say,

> *"Godly people give generously to the poor. Their deeds will never be forgotten."* 2 CORINTHIANS 9:9

Even more, "Whoever gives to the poor will lack nothing. But a curse will come upon those who close their eyes to poverty" (Proverbs 28:27).

Do you see the pattern here? God promises to bless those who store their treasure in heaven by being generous to others—in particular, the poor. People who insist on hoarding treasure on earth will not experience God's blessing. But don't just be generous for generosity's sake. Guard your heart. Make sure you are giving in order to gain God's approval, not to impress others or to quietly congratulate yourself. Giving to God means just that—giving Him all you have so you will become all that He wants you to be.

- If you never have enough at the end of the month, perhaps you aren't giving God enough at the beginning.

- No matter how hard you try, you can't outgive God.

- Be generous in what you give, but never take pride in it. A proud heart trumps a generous heart every time.

- It's not the size of the check that counts; it's the condition of the heart.

- God doesn't need your money, but He knows you need to give your money.

The real problem is not why
some pious, humble, believing people suffer,
but why some do not.

C. S. Lewis

TWENTY-FIVE

THE PROBLEM OF PAIN

We all suffer pain, but it varies in kind and degree. It might be physical—an acute discomfort in some area of your body, caused by a violent injury or a severe illness. Or it might be emotional—an extreme distress or heartbreak over some problem or circumstance. Whether it is physiological or emotional, all pain has something in common: It hurts!

Many of us have an immature understanding of pain. We haven't studied it or even thought about it at length. We certainly don't want to take time to analyze our pain while we are experiencing it; it hurts so much, we just want to get rid of it as soon as possible. We don't want to dwell on it a moment longer than necessary. Thus, the ramifications of pain are left unexplored. Because both types of pain "hurt," we mistakenly assume that the principles of dealing with one also apply to the other.

This lack of understanding can be dangerous because our judgment is impaired while we endure the agony of our pain. Normal reactions to pain are that it hurts, it's a bad thing, and it should be avoided. But these typical responses aren't necessarily correct. In fact, a proper understanding of pain is counterintuitive—you have to think past your initial knee-jerk reaction to it. For example:

> *Initial reaction:* Pain is detrimental.
> *Proper reaction:* Pain can be beneficial.

Physical pain can be an early warning signal of a more severe undiagnosed problem. If you didn't have the pain, you wouldn't know to get an examination. There is a similar benefit to emotional pain—if your pain is the result of the way you have treated others, it becomes a deterrent to repeating that offensive behavior.

> *Initial reaction:* Pain is proof that something went
> wrong.

Proper reaction: Pain can be the consequence of a
   correct action.

If an engaged couple breaks up and calls off a wedding, there will be pain. The sense of hurt is natural and understandable, but it doesn't mean the decision was wrong. If the two people were not truly in love or compatible with each other, a subsequent divorce would be far worse than the pain of breaking an engagement.

Initial reaction: Pain will subside with the passage
   of time.
Proper reaction: A cause may need to be rectified
   before the pain can be alleviated.

The initial reaction is true for a bump on the head or a stubbed toe. But it won't apply if the cause of the pain is a cancerous tumor. Time alone will not fix this pain—corrective surgery is required. Similarly, with emotional pain, the passage of time may serve as a distraction—but a reconciliation may be necessary for the pain to be permanently relieved.

Initial reaction: Pain is to be avoided at all costs.

Proper reaction: You shouldn't live in fear of pain.

Okay, avoidance of physical pain is good if it keeps you from testing the law of aerodynamics by jumping off your roof with a handkerchief for a parachute. But don't try to insulate yourself from emotional pain by living an introspective existence. For your spiritual and emotional well-being, you need to be involved in the lives of other people. Some of these relationships may occasionally result in pain—but in others you will discover real meaning and purpose for your life.

Pain can be a good thing. God designed it that way. Don't be so focused on the hurt of pain that you overlook the help of it.

- You are apt to learn more from pain than from pleasure.

- Those who appreciate life the most are those who have experienced the most pain.

- The challenge is to endure pain without being one to the people around you.

- Pain will reveal the strength of your faith—or the lack of it.

- You can only suffer the pain of loss if you have loved.

Never let the sense of past failure
defeat your next step.

Oswald Chambers

TWENTY-SIX

DISILLUSIONMENT, DESPAIR, AND DEPRESSION

There is an ache that afflicts the human heart that has nothing to do with disease or death. It's a heaviness that comes when we are disillusioned, despairing, or depressed. Though it is possible to function with anxiety or concern weighing upon us, we can't function *normally*. Life becomes burdensome when we are dominated by negative feelings and thoughts, and we begin to doubt the promise of hope.

One way to look at disillusionment, despair, and depression is to see them as avenues back to the heart of God. God doesn't necessarily *cause* these afflictions, but He can *use* them to bring us closer to Him. Here's what we mean.

Have you ever been disillusioned over a person you think should have acted differently? Why the disillusionment? It came because your preconceived notion about that person turned out to be false. In other words, it was an *illusion*. To be *dis*-illusioned is to see people as they really are, which can trigger a negative response in us. Don't let that happen. Never place unrealistic demands on people, especially the people you care most about. They will never be able to live up to your expectations. Instead, place your expectations on God. He is the only one who can satisfy them. With God there are no illusions.

When it comes to despair, there are generally two causes. The first is a sense of having done something you can't change, as much as you'd like to. Maybe you did something you think is terrible—and you don't see how you could possibly move on. You said something you can't take back, you did something you can't undo, or you caused something you can't change. The other cause for despair comes from not doing something you believe you should have. Perhaps you missed a great opportunity, or you didn't say something you should have. Either cause—doing something you shouldn't have, or not doing something you should have—can easily lead to despair.

Rather than living in your despair, give it to God. If you need to ask God to forgive you, do it now. Admit your mistake, accept His forgiveness, and move on. If you regret missing an opportunity, don't dwell on it. Pick yourself up and find the next opportunity.

Despair is a common human experience. It shows we are unable to do the right thing all the time. But it's also a wake-up call for us to break from the past and trust God for the future.

Depression seems more deep-seated and less easily overcome than disillusionment and despair. Yet God can use our depression to help us appreciate life's ordinary things. Without depression, we would never appreciate joy. Like a piece of black velvet that makes a diamond sparkle, depression can lead us to exult in life's natural treasures. A floral bouquet, a baby's smile, a vivid sunset—these are the kinds of things that can bring us to a place of happiness once again.

The key is not simply to try to overcome our depression, but to rest in God's provision and strength. When the prophet Elijah was so depressed that he wanted to die, God sent an angel who encouraged Elijah to eat. When the apostle Paul felt crushed and overwhelmed by all the hard stuff in his life, he learned to rely on God rather than himself. "And he did deliver us from mortal danger," Paul writes. "And we are confident that he will continue to deliver us" (2 Corinthians 1:10).

More than anything else, God desires that we love Him with every part of our being: heart, soul, mind, and strength. If any of these are weak, He is the one to give us strength. He is the one who will give us hope.

- While we sometimes live in the past, God always pulls us to the future.

- The only thing in the world you can change is *you*.

- God is more eager to forgive than we are willing to ask forgiveness.

- The best cure for depression is hope.

- The best source of hope is God.

Yet what we suffer now
is nothing compared to the glory
he [God] will give us later.

Romans 8:18

TWENTY-SEVEN

DEALING WITH A CHRONIC ILLNESS

Most sicknesses are an inconvenience: Your nose is runny, so you search desperately for a Kleenex, or the flu keeps you home and you miss shopping at the Saturday yard sales. (Actually, many husbands fake flu symptoms for this very reason.) Even most occasions for hospitalization are mundane: The staff is usually attentive to you, then you spend a few days in bed at home recovering; you may get bored with watching television, but sooner or later you'll be back on your feet. There may be some physical discomfort, an interrupted schedule, and, ultimately, medical bills to cover, but most health issues are temporary and manageable.

Not so with chronic illness—the physical maladies that just won't go away. And they don't get better. You are stuck dealing with pain and problems on a continual basis. It is a situation you face twenty-four hours a day, 365 days a year, times the number of years left in your life. This prospect is simply depressing if you allow yourself to think any further ahead than one day at a time.

What can you do if forced to deal with chronic problems for which there is no relief? Is it possible to endure reality when real life is continually brutal? There is only one solution: You have to live outside the physical realm.

We aren't trying to get philosophical or abstract here. We aren't advocating transcendence to a higher state of consciousness or the denial of reality for a mystical state of being. We are simply suggesting that you focus on the spiritual dimension of life.

God created humanity with a spiritual component. Here is how King Solomon, acknowledged to be the wisest man who ever lived, described it:

> *He* [God] *has planted eternity in the human heart.*
>
> ECCLESIASTES 3:11

God's existence is undeniable as we instinctively sense His presence all around us; in our hearts, we perceive the invisible qualities of His eternal power and divine nature, as the apostle Paul once wrote to the church in Rome:

> *For the truth about God is known to them instinctively. God has put this knowledge in their hearts. From the time the world was created, people have seen the earth and sky and all that God made. They can clearly see his invisible qualitites—his eternal power and divine nature.* ROMANS 1:19–20

We have been designed with a void in our lives that only God can fill. We can choose to deny it, but we are incomplete when we do.

Because God operates in the spiritual dimension of our lives, it is at that level we build a relationship with Him. Yes, there are tangible and physical expressions of our worship, and there are physical manifestations of His involvement in the world. But our primary relationship with Him will be in the spiritual realm.

As our focus becomes more spiritual, our thoughts are occupied with things eternal. We are less absorbed with matters that are temporal. Our spiritual perspective doesn't make reality any less real, but it puts it into the context of God's paradigm. For Him, our life on earth is as fleeting as a vapor.

Nothing can be said to diminish chronic pain. But while immediate physical relief may not be possible, the despair of dealing with constant pain may be overcome by the hope found in the spiritual realm. Only God has the power to draw your thoughts out of this world while you are still living in it.

- Chronic pain may be with you for a lifetime. God will be with you for eternity.

- God may not choose to change your circumstances, but He promises to change your perspective about them.

- When you need a change of scenery from your situation, spend time with the only One who is out of this world.

- God isn't asking you to deny reality. But He does want you to view it from a spiritual perspective.

- They don't call God's Spirit "the Comforter" for nothing. Allow Him to show you how He got that name.

Illness is a convent which has
its rule, its austerity,
its silences, and its inspirations.

Albert Camus

TWENTY-EIGHT

CONFRONTED WITH CANCER

Cancer—the word nobody likes to hear. From a technical standpoint, cancer is a change in the normal growth of cells, causing them to spread and destroy healthy tissues and organs of the body. But from an emotional perspective, cancer is one of the most devastating pronouncements a person and his or her family can receive. It's not exactly a death sentence, but that's the first thing many people think when a medical professional gives them the news.

Thanks to advances in research and development, many types of cancer that were virtually incurable several years ago are now very treatable—if caught early enough. So there is reason for hope. Still, cancer can be devastating to a family. If you, a member of your family, or a close friend is suffering from cancer right now, you understand what we're talking about. It isn't easy to confront, and it can't always be beaten. But it doesn't have to get the best of you.

You learn a lot about people when they come face-to-face with the life and death Ping-Pong struggle of a dreaded disease. Over the last few years we've watched a half dozen family members and close friends battle cancer. Although each one had a different form of the disease, they shared much in common—primarily the fact that all were people of faith. It didn't matter whether they had a modest or vital relationship with God when they first received their diagnosis. As their treatment—and in some cases, the disease—progressed, so did their connection with God. Though they suffered from the physical effects of the disease and the potency of the treatment, the immaterial part of their being gained strength.

> *That is why we never give up. Though our bodies are dying, our spirits are being renewed every day.*
> 2 CORINTHIANS 4:16

One friend who had always been a driven, successful businessman fought valiantly against a brain tumor. When his cancer prevented him from working daily, he took calls at home, mostly to encourage his coworkers. In the final few months, colleagues, friends, and family came to his side—at home or in the hospital. They came to offer the few words of encouragement they could muster, and invariably, they left feeling as though *they* were the ones who had been blessed.

A family member with a cancer that responded successfully to treatment began sending e-mails to a network of people who had committed to pray for him. Those of us who received his messages looked forward to reading them, filled as they were with praise to God.

> *For our present troubles are quite small and won't last*
> *very long. Yet they produce for us an immeasurably*
> *great glory that will last forever!*
>
> 2 CORINTHIANS 4:17

A friend who struggled with breast cancer was tireless in her efforts to find the best doctors and course of treatment. Like so many cancer patients, her family gave her incredible support. When she lost her hair due to chemotherapy, her husband told everyone she was more beautiful than ever. He set up a prayer network and reported specific needs so we could all pray.

Regardless of the outcomes, each one of our friends and family members who battled cancer gave us a glimpse of eternity. Some have passed on to the ultimate pain-free, disease-free, and stress-free life with God, while others are thanking their Creator for more years here on earth. For the latter, even in recovery, they seem to hold on to that connection to the eternal, knowing that for all of us, it's just a matter of time before we experience what God has prepared for those who love Him.

So we don't look at the troubles we can see right now;
rather, we look forward to what we have not yet seen.
For the troubles we see will soon be over, but the joys to
come will last forever.   2 CORINTHIANS 4:18

- The human spirit's ability to find good in tragedy is a gift from God.

- Only those who have had cancer understand that even a deadly disease can bring blessings.

- The condition of the body has little or no relationship to the condition of the spirit.

- The next time you visit a cancer patient, prepare to be inspired.

- The best thing you can do for someone experiencing the hard stuff of cancer is to offer encouragement and prayer.

T he whole point of this life
is the healing of the heart's eye
through which God is seen.

St. Augustine

TWENTY-NINE

DOES GOD STILL HEAL?

While He lived on this earth, Jesus Christ was known for many things. He was a spellbinding teacher, He performed wondrous miracles, and He spoke many dramatic prophecies. As He traveled throughout His home region of Galilee, Jesus also "healed people who had every kind of sickness and disease" (Matthew 4:23). Healing was an important part of the ministry of Jesus. Beyond simply curing the diseases and deformities of people, the miraculous healings of Jesus authenticated His divine nature.

When Jesus healed—like the time He opened the ears and loosed the tongue of a man born deaf and mute—the large crowd that followed Him was amazed. Again and again the people said, "Everything he does is wonderful" (Mark 7:37). Eventually, the people became preoccupied with Christ's healing power. Whenever He entered a region, the word would spread and the sick would come, desperate for a healing touch.

It's no different today. There's not a sick person who doesn't desire healing. Most people rely on the expertise and care of medical doctors, whose expert diagnosis, correct prescriptions, and gifted hands often bring wholeness to our wounded bodies, emotions, and minds. Other people go directly to God—or to a minister of God—and ask for miraculous healing. No doubt you've seen the parades of people on television shows putting their hope in so-called "faith healers." Perhaps you have attended such a meeting with the hope that God would heal you.

Does God still heal? Jesus isn't here among us physically to perform His miracles, but He is with us spiritually—and He is certainly capable of healing bodies, minds, and emotions. After all, He made them!

If God still heals, does He use the skills of the medical community exclusively, or does He work through the promises of faith healers? Or does God utilize a variety of methods?

To get to the heart of healing, we need to go back to Jesus. Yes, physical healing was an important part of His earthly ministry, but Jesus had more than the *physical* in mind when He healed people.

> *"Healthy people don't need a doctor—sick people do. I*
> *have come to call sinners, not those who think they are*
> *already good enough."*　　　　　　MARK 2:17

Jesus was the Great Physician because He healed both physical and *spiritual* sickness. The good news for us is that Jesus still does that today. There is no sickness or sin problem He can't handle.

> *Praise the LORD, I tell myself, and never forget the*
> *good things he does for me. He forgives all my sins and*
> *heals all my diseases.*　　　　　　PSALM 103:2–3

When we or someone we love is facing an illness, we need to remember that the most important healing touch anyone can receive is spiritual. Whenever Jesus healed, that was always His first concern. In fact, focusing too much on the physical can distract us from the most important issue—our spiritual condition. Yes, God still heals physically, but that's not His primary concern. Because we will be completely healed in heaven, God's bigger concern is that we get there.

- No doctor is a god, but God can use doctors to accomplish His purposes.

- It's possible to become so preoccupied with your physical health that you neglect your spiritual health.

- The person who doesn't think God can heal doesn't think much of God.

- If you focus too much on earthly things, your hurts will get the best of you.

- If you always keep heaven in mind, you will think less about healing and more about the Healer.

You are the light of the world—
like a city on a mountain,
glowing in the night for all to see."

THIRTY

ALL WILL BE WELL

Recently we took part in a healing service for a dear friend with a deadly brain tumor. He was scheduled for surgery, so a few close friends, including two ministers, gathered at his home. One of the ministers read a well-known passage from the New Testament book of James:

> *Are any among you sick? They should call for the elders*
> *of the church and have them pray over them, anointing*
> *them with oil in the name of the Lord. And their*
> *prayer offered in faith will heal the sick, and the Lord*
> *will make them well.*   JAMES 5:14–15

Then the other minister anointed our friend with oil, and we all prayed for God's healing. None of us had any doubts that God *could* heal our friend. Still, there were those of who wondered if God *would* heal him.

The surgery was performed, and the outlook was grim. We continued to pray, hoping for a miracle—but it was not to be. Within five months our friend had passed into eternity. There was sadness, of course, but there was also hope. Though God had not healed our friend physically, He had actually done much more.

We know this because we visited our friend one month before he died. Physically, he was deteriorating, but there was a sparkle in his eye. As we talked, we asked if he was disappointed that God had not healed him. "Oh, but He has," our friend replied, sitting up as straight as he could. "God has healed me in ways you can't imagine. I don't want you to worry about me. God is in control. All will be well."

Then he handed us this prayer which he personalized from Mother Teresa:

Dear Jesus,
Help me to spread Your fragrance everywhere I go.
Flood my soul with Your spirit and life.

Penetrate and possess my whole being so utterly
that my life may only be a radiance of Yours.

Shine through me and be so in me,
that every soul I come in contact with
may feel Your presence in my soul.

Let them look up and see
no longer me, but only Jesus!

Stay with me
and I shall begin to shine as You shine;
so to shine as to be a light to others;
the light, O Jesus, will be all from You.

None of it will be mine;
it will be You shining on others through me.

Let me thus praise You in the way You love best,
by shining on those around me.

Let me preach You without preaching,
not by words but example,
by the catching force,
the sympathetic influence
of what I do,
the evident fullness of the love
my heart bears to You.

Amen.[2]

"This is how God has healed me," our friend said. "He is using my life to touch others with His love. As long as I live, I want God to use me."

Indeed, God used our friend to shine on hundreds of people who saw him in the last weeks of his life. God had healed him, and through that healing, God showed us how much He cares for us all. God demonstrated that our prayers were not empty. As the healing passage in James concludes, our prayers had "great power and wonderful results" (James 5:16).

- God promises to bless those who mourn, though He never promises to remove our mourning.

- Prayer is the way we engage God's healing power.

- The light of Jesus never fades even though our bodies do.

- A life given over to God is a powerful thing.

- There's no such thing as an empty prayer.

Everyone has noticed how hard it is
to turn our thoughts to God when
everything is going well with us.
We "have all we want" is a terrible saying
when "all" does not include God.

C. S. Lewis

THIRTY-ONE

HEARING GOD

One of the great lies of humanism is that all suffering is bad. The skeptic—that is, the one who doubts that God exists—argues that suffering demonstrates there is no all-good and all-powerful God in charge of this world. If there were such a God, the skeptic says, He would not allow suffering of any kind.

The problem with this argument is that in the practical world of human experience (as opposed to the theoretical world of academic reasoning), we know better. While no one looks forward to pain and suffering, and no one wants to see it inflicted on others, there is no denying that suffering can be helpful. Indeed, you could say that rather than separating us from God, suffering does a pretty good job of pointing us toward Him.

In a perfect world, of course, suffering doesn't belong. God created this world to be perfect, and there was no such thing as suffering. After He finished His creation, God pronounced it "good." Then sin entered the world, marring the goodness. It wasn't that God had lost control or interest in His world. Sin was allowed to enter because He created us with the capacity to freely choose (or reject) Him. The effect of sin was dramatic, for with it came physical and spiritual death. But there was yet another consequence. In the words of Peter Kreeft, sin "made us stupid, so that we can only learn the hard way."

It would be great if, in our present state, we could follow God and learn wisdom and virtue in a pain-free environment. But the fact of the matter is that we are fallen creatures—and most of the time we are drawn to God only when things aren't going well. In his book *The Problem of Pain*, C. S. Lewis addresses this idea head-on. He refers to pain as "God's megaphone," serving the purpose of getting our attention. He writes:

> No doubt Pain as God's megaphone is a terrible
> instrument; it may lead to final and unrepented

rebellion. But it gives the only opportunity the bad man
can have for amendment. It removes the veil; it plants
the flag of truth within the fortress of a rebel soul.

Have you found that true in your own life? Did you first surrender to God because your life was in great shape or because you were in the midst of crisis? Are you drawn closer to God now when things go well or when you experience difficulties? It's easy to put God off when things are going well, because who really needs Him then? As St. Augustine said, "God wants to give us something, but cannot, because our hands are full—there's nowhere for Him to put it."

Truth is, when we experience pain and suffering, we are much more in tune to God—not because God enjoys our trials, but because He delights in getting us through them. Not only can we hear God's voice more clearly through our pain, but we long to hear Him. What does He want from us? What does He have for us? How about courage and strength? How about truth and wisdom? How about patience and a clearer understanding of the way things really are in the world? As Kreeft writes, "It seems that everything that has intrinsic value, everything that cannot be bought or negotiated, or compromised or relativized or reduced, goes with suffering."

Unless you make it a point to hear God, the hard stuff in your life will seem random and meaningless. On the other hand, when you seek God and listen to His voice, your present troubles will draw you closer to Him. There, safe in His arms, you may not get all the answers you're looking for—but you will find meaning in the midst of your pain.

- In the midst of your pain, opening your ears to God will automatically open your heart.

- There was a time in this world when pain and suffering did not exist. Someday that time will return.

- God has never lost interest in this world, and He never will.

- Our suffering matters to God. It matters so much that He subjected His own Son to the worst kind.

- If you can't hear God in the hard stuff of your life, it's unlikely you will hear Him in the good stuff.

G rief is the agony of an instant,
the indulgence of grief the blunder of a life.

Benjamin Disraeli

THIRTY-TWO

GOOD GRIEF

Grief. Just the mention of the word conjures up visions of a funeral home and cemetery. Even the dictionary makes the connection—"Grief: a noun meaning intense and profound sadness, especially as a result of a death."

Grief is a word that is familiar to everyone, though no one wants to experience it. Yet we all do—at one time or another. It is inescapable. And as such, it is natural. So why is it that some people who have a deep faith in God are ashamed to acknowledge grief?

- Is it a sign of weak faith when we grieve over the loss of a loved one?

- Does our grief suggest that we don't trust God with the circumstances of our lives?
- Is grief the telltale sign that we lack faith in the "life after death" that God has promised?
- Is our sadness evidence of doubt?

The Bible teaches that those who believe in God have a spiritual and eternal hope. For them, this life is not all there is. In fact, for them death is the end of their sorrow and pain; the end of this life is just the beginning of life everlasting.

But the Bible doesn't suggest that those who believe in God are insulated from grief. To the contrary, it states that those who believe in God will grieve. Scripture does, however, make the distinction that they will not grieve in the same way as those who have no faith.

Here's the distinction: Faith in God involves hope. A hope in the future. The hope of a better life yet to come. A hope of spending eternity with our heavenly Father. This "hope" is not simply a wishful feeling for a desirable event (as in "I hope I win the lottery" or "I hope the restaurant isn't out of key lime pie"). In the faith context, *hope* is the certainty of an anticipated event. It is a confident knowledge of a future circumstance based on the character and promises of God Himself.

Those who have no faith in God lack this hope. And when there is no hope, death brings despair. Death triggers grief in those who remain. That marks the difference. Faith doesn't eliminate grief, but it does change it qualitatively:

- *Without faith,* there is total despair in grief. This present life is as good as it gets. In fact, this life is all there ever is. Death represents the total finality—and futility—of it all. Death is to be feared.

- *With faith,* there is hope even in the face of death. This present life is as bad as it will ever get. Things only get better—perfect in fact—when the present life ends. Death represents the beginning of a celestial celebration. Death is a step in the process of getting nearer to God.

God does not expect us to be jubilant at funerals. Yes, the eternal prospect for a person whose faith was in God is worth celebrating. But God knows we will mourn the temporary loss of love and companionship. So He has no complaint with your grief. But don't let your sorrow overshadow the hope that exists for those who believe in God. Don't let the sadness of the temporal obscure your assurance of things eternal.

There is an appropriate time and place for your grief. Anytime and anyplace—whenever and wherever you experience the sense of loss. It is an honest emotion that should not be denied or stifled. You are no less spiritual because you are sad. Just don't let your sadness turn to despair. Instead, make your sadness sacred—recognize that it is temporary in the context of God's eternity.

- There is hope in your future if God is in your present.

- Faith in God changes the meaning of death. It no longer signals the end—it marks the beginning.

- Grief without God's presence ends in despair. Grief with God by your side is no less painful, but ends with hope.

- For those who believe in God, death brings an end to sorrow and pain. The sadness of those left to mourn is diminished when they celebrate this fact.

- Grief is an expression of your love. Your hope in the midst of grief is an expression of God's love.

—————————————

Jesus loves the little children,
All the children of the world.
Red and yellow, black and white,
They are precious in His sight;
Jesus loves the little children of the world.

—————————————

Children's chorus

THIRTY-THREE

WHEN CHILDREN SUFFER

Of all the hard stuff we observe in the world, the most incomprehensible is the suffering of children.

If it's your own child hurting, you will do anything to ease the pain. A father was holding his newborn baby when someone asked, "Would you throw yourself in front of a car to save him?" Without hesitation he replied, "Absolutely!" Although the father had known his child for just a few days, the bond was permanently set. We will do anything to protect our children and to keep them from harm.

Even when we observe the suffering of other children—the poor and starving in Africa or young ones afflicted with disease in our own land—our hearts melt. What can be done? Who'll stop their pain?

Much is being done to bring relief to these little ones. If we are so inclined, we can join the heroic efforts of organizations such as World Vision and Compassion International, who help millions of children around the globe every day. It's not unusual for a church to sponsor hundreds of orphaned children from a single village, where hunger and disease have devastated the adult population. Where they once fought a daily battle for survival, these children now have food, clothing, shelter, an education—and hope. Hundreds of children out of millions who are suffering may seem like a drop in the proverbial bucket, but it is a start.

On our own continent, we may not see suffering on the same scale, but our hearts break for little ones whose bodies are ravaged by cancer and other cruel diseases. Maybe you are experiencing something like that in your own family, or perhaps you know someone whose child is fighting for his or her life. It's a hard thing to watch because the children seem so helpless. Yet we must not give up hope, for just when we wonder if anything can be done for these kids, we see the outstanding and tireless work of research organizations, such as the Muscular Dystrophy Association, in seeking a cure for these childhood maladies.

Mattie Stepanek, the bright-eyed boy with muscular dystrophy who died weeks before his fourteenth birthday, became an eloquent advocate for all hurting children when he began writing to cope with his own struggle. His stirring poems, prayers, essays, and stories on topics like grief, love, disability, and peace became anthems for a world touched by the resilience of one whose physical condition never dimmed his spirit. Who can forget his bright eyes and knowing smile, especially when he recited one of his touching poems, which he called "heartsongs"?

We may hurt over the pain the children of the world experience, but we must never forget that God holds them in His hand. When Jesus walked the earth, He invited the children to come to Him, even when it wasn't convenient, or when bigger issues seemed to press upon Him. Once some parents brought their children to Jesus so He could touch them and bless them, but His disciples didn't think He had time for the little ones. Jesus reprimanded them by saying,

> *"Let the children come to me. Don't stop them! For the Kingdom of God belongs to such as these. I assure you, anyone who doesn't have their kind of faith will never get into the Kingdom of God."* MARK 10:14–15

Then Jesus picked up the children, held them in His arms, and blessed them by placing His hands on their heads. That's how much He loves the children, all the children of the world.

Despite our best efforts to provide relief and to help find a cure for those children who are hurting and who need a healing touch—and these efforts should never stop—we must remember that God's mercy and grace never go away, and sometimes they shine brightest through the weakest of vessels. The lessons we learn from all children, especially those who are suffering, should make us better people and our world a better place.

- When we are weak, God is strong.

- The tears of a hurting child should bring us to tears.

- Don't let the needs of the world overwhelm you—let them motivate you.

- Teach your own children about the needs of other children. You will be surprised at how much they can do.

- There's not a child in the world God doesn't know by name, and there's not a child who God doesn't love more than anything else.

It is one of the mysteries of our nature that man,
all unprepared, can receive
a thunder stroke [of bad news] and live.
There is but one reasonable explanation of it.
The intellect is stunned by the shock
and but gropingly gathers the meaning of the words.
The power to realize their full import is mercifully lacking.

Mark Twain
(on receiving news of the death of a loved one)

THIRTY-FOUR

GOING FROM HURTING TO HEALING

Writing this book focused our thoughts on the many tragedies that occur in life. Each one is different and—for the lives affected—very personal. While we would never attempt to prioritize hardships according to severity, we are struck by the disruption caused by an unexpected death. Whether caused by an unpredicted heart attack, a car accident, or murder, the death of a loved one leaves you hanging. . .without warning, so many things are left unsaid. There's not even a chance to say a simple good-bye.

It occurred to us that someone with particular insights on premature death might be the county coroner. The occasion of our visit occurred on the one-year anniversary of a multiple murder investigated by her and the rest of the coroner's staff. In a tragedy defying imagination, nine related women and children, living in a single household, had been shot to death.

We wondered how a professional investigator deals with the abject horror of such a situation. Does she become calloused and insensitive over time? Can she remove the thoughts from her mind when she returns home? Is she ever able to shake the specter of death? She answered all of our questions by stating the philosophy of her office: On the technical side, it is the coroner's job to determine the cause of death; but on the human and emotional side, it is the role of her office to help survivors deal with their loss. She concluded her comments to us by saying, "We try to make a good thing out of a bad thing."

The lesson we learned from the county coroner may help you deal with catastrophes that happen in your world. Her advice can apply whether you are directly affected by a tragedy within your family, or are the friend of a person impacted by a disastrous event. When misfortune strikes, look for an opportunity to make a positive difference in another person's life. Look for those who are hurting—even though you may be grieving yourself. Consider how the sadness of the situation can be alleviated—even just a bit—by some kindness on your part. Consider that your role in restoring these people involves moving them from a place of hurting to a place of healing.

This perspective is not limited to occurrences of death. It can apply to all the hard stuff in life. The misfortune that strikes someone's life could be physical, in many ways other than death—a chronic illness, a compulsive eating disorder, or a diagnosis of Alzheimer's disease. Or the adversity could be emotional—living in a difficult marriage, dealing with a rebellious child, or facing myriad other antagonistic relationships. Or the hardship could be financial—the loss of a job, a broken-down car without money to fix it, or the constant strain of debt with the accompanying worry that there won't be enough money for rent and groceries.

These are the situations happening all around you. And even if you find yourself in the middle of the storm, there are many others affected, too. So change your perspective. Don't focus on the tragedy; that will only make you morose. And don't think only about how you are impacted; that will make you self-centered. Look at the others who are hurting. Commit yourself to the noble effort of making a difference in their lives. Endeavor to make good out of a bad thing. Do whatever it takes to move them from a place of hurting to a place of healing. Don't assume that others will do it. Take on the responsibility yourself. The person you help will be better for what you have done. And so will you.

- Don't turn away from a tragedy. Consider it an opportunity to make a positive difference in someone's life.

- Look for opportunities to caringly move someone who is hurting to a place of healing.

- You can't stop hard things from happening. But you can work to achieve some good result in a bad situation.

- Even if you are the one suffering, don't forget that others are hurting, too.

- The best thing you can do for yourself in *your* grief is to help other people in *theirs*.

In that day the wolf and lamb will live together;
the leopard and the goat will be at peace.
Calves and yearlings will be safe among lions,
and a little child will lead them all.

Isaiah 11:6

THIRTY-FIVE

WILL YOUR PET BE IN HEAVEN?

One of the most beautiful pictures of God's glorious future kingdom—where there will be everlasting peace, beauty, and goodness—is the complete harmony among the animals. Here on earth, there is anything but harmony. Wild animals' interactions are generally "eat or be eaten." Even our domesticated animals don't always get along.

As for our relationship with the animals, it's not exactly ideal, either. Though God commanded us to care for the animals, we don't always do a very good job. Still, one of God's great blessings is the pleasure animals bring us. We enjoy their beauty and admire their ability to survive in the wild. And when we adopt an animal and care for it in our home, we literally consider that pet a part of the family.

When an animal suffers, we feel its pain—so much so that we have enacted laws to prevent cruelty to animals. And when we lose a pet, we are sometimes surprised at the emotions that well up inside. Which leads us to the big question: What happens to an animal when it dies?

As you could predict, there are differing views on this issue. One says that when an animal dies, it ceases to exist. There's no possibility of an afterlife for animals because animals do not have an eternal, spiritual nature. Proponents of this view emphasize the differences between animals and people; though God created all living things, only human beings were created in His image. Here's the way it happened:

> *Then God said, "Let us make people in our image, to be*
> *like ourselves. They will be masters over all life—the*
> *fish in the sea, the birds in the sky, and all the livestock,*
> *wild animals, and small animals."* GENESIS 1:26

Because we are made in God's image, we possess qualities

that animals don't. For example, we have a moral code built inside, giving us the sense of right and wrong. Animals, on the other hand, function by instinct. Furthermore, we have the ability to learn, reason, and use language in ways that animals can't. And we have an immaterial, spiritual dimension that enables us to relate personally to God. We can pray to God, praise Him, and hear Him speak to us. No animal has ever had that ability.

It is this spiritual part of humankind that lasts forever. Though our bodies die, our spirits continue to exist. Without a spiritual dimension, some say, animals cannot live forever. When their bodies die, they simply cease to exist. The conclusion of this view is that there will be no animals in heaven, at least not the animals we have known on earth.

Of course, that isn't the only view. Another perspective presents a different picture. While agreeing that there is a spiritual difference between humans and animals, this view allows for the presence of animals in heaven. We see from scripture that animals will be part of God's kingdom on earth, so why couldn't they be in heaven? If there will be other nonhuman living things in heaven (such as green fields and flowers), why not animals?

But what about specific animals, such as your pet? The Bible doesn't speak to the question, so we can only speculate. Certainly, with God all things are possible. If He wanted to raise up your pet in the last days so that you might be reunited in heaven, He could. The focus of heaven will be our worship of Jesus Christ, the Lamb of God, but that doesn't necessarily exclude ordinary lambs or dogs or cats or other animals that could add to the supreme pleasure heaven promises.

In the meantime, we are to care for our animals just as we care for each other. This is what God does (see Psalm 36:6), and as creatures made in His image, we are to imitate Him in all we do.

- As the scriptures say, the godly care for their animals.

- Animals were created for us to use—not misuse.

- One of the biggest reasons we love animals is that they don't judge us.

- Animals may not share certain capacities with us, such as the ability to reason, but there's one thing we do share: the capacity to suffer.

- Animals make us better humans.

They've been at the bedside,
watching someone they love in agony
as cancer nipped at the spine,
as the chest rose and fell with
the cruel mimicry of the respirator,
as the music of personality dwindled to
a single note and then fell silent.
They know life when they see it,
and they know it when it is gone.

Anna Quindlen

THIRTY-SIX

WHEN A PARENT GOES HOME

Death is inevitable. We all know that. But the inescapability and certainty of death don't make it any easier to endure when you are watching a loved one slip away.

In the usual chronological order of life, it is the plight of an adult child to witness the death of a parent. When it happens quickly and unexpectedly, the survivors regret the missed opportunity to have said good-bye; they were deprived of one last occasion to reaffirm to their parent the appreciation and love that marked their relationship. But a more torturous circumstance befalls the adult child who must sit by the bedside of a parent whose life fades away slowly, over days or weeks or months. For these brave men and women, the battle is not a medical one on behalf of their parent; rather, their greatest fight is often an internal one. Of course, there is a part of them that hopes for their parent's complete physical recovery; but faced with reality and the inevitability of death, they often wonder if it is appropriate to pray for God to relieve the suffering by speeding the process along. Why must their parent's anguish be prolonged? Can't God, in His mercy, bring a gentle halt to the prolonged torment of an already depleted life? These are honest and heartfelt questions, but many people never ask them out loud—because they feel guilty over the silent thoughts in their minds.

God's timing in matters of death transcends our understanding. We may doubt His wisdom when life continues in a body or mind that otherwise seems dead. But the same kind of questions arise when a life ends much sooner than we think appropriate. Such was the case some two thousand years ago when the sisters Mary and Martha were concerned for their sick brother, Lazarus. They sent word to their close family friend, Jesus, that Lazarus was close to death. They were confident that Lazarus could hang on to life for the short time that it would take Jesus to travel to their home and perform one of His well-known healing miracles. But upon receiving news of Lazarus's grave condition, Jesus did something strange: He delayed His journey to Lazarus's hometown for several days. By the time Jesus arrived in

Bethany, Lazarus had died and been buried for more than half a week. This unexplained and obviously unnecessary delay prompted Martha to say to Jesus:

> *"Lord, if you had been here, my brother would not have died."*
> JOHN 11:21

But this story doesn't end with mourners wailing at Lazarus's gravesite. Jesus walked up to the cave in which Lazarus had been buried, prayed, and then shouted, "Lazarus, come out!" And that's exactly what happened as life returned to Lazarus's corpse. He walked out of the tomb still wrapped in burial cloths.

As excited as Mary and Martha must have been to see their brother resurrected, they no doubt wondered about God's sense of timing. Wouldn't it have been better for Jesus to have healed Lazarus during his sickness? Why allow death to occur, with its accompanying grief and sadness? Think of the emotional turmoil that could have been avoided had Jesus arrived while Lazarus still lived. Does this suggest that God is indifferent to the emotional trauma of humanity, and unconcerned with our feelings?

We do have a clue about God's timing in the story of

Lazarus. Jesus intentionally delayed His journey to Bethany, telling His disciples that Lazarus was not the featured person in the events that were about to unfold. Rather, the miracle they would soon see in Bethany would be "for the glory of God" (John 11:4).

And so it is with circumstances that surround a lingering death. Like Mary and Martha, we may not understand God's timing —but that doesn't mean that God is removed from, ignorant of, or indifferent to the situation. He is in the middle of it all. Comfort will not be gained by trying to understand God's timing, but consolation is ours when we acknowledge that God controls the timing.

- The death of a loved one is always tragic, but we must trust God's timing in it all.

- In matters of life and death, God knows best.

- Appreciate your life; let others know you cherish theirs.

- God is the Designer, Creator, and Sustainer of life. With those credentials, shouldn't we trust Him with decisions about the end of life?

- For those who know God, death is the doorway through which we pass to enter into God's presence. It is not something to be avoided; it is to be anxiously anticipated.

G od blesses those who mourn,
for they will be comforted."

Matthew 5:4

THIRTY-SEVEN

GRIEF IN STAGES

As people made in God's image, we have a sense of eternity planted in our hearts (Ecclesiastes 3:11). Still, we grieve when something we care deeply about ceases to exist. It may be a spouse, a friend, a parent, or a pet. The loss may concern a project, a cause, or a candidate. When the people and things that matter most to us are no longer around, the same feelings of grief can well up inside of us, causing mental, emotional, spiritual, and even physical distress.

Grief is nothing to be ashamed of—it's part of the human existence and experience. So when something you love is taken away, the question should not be, "Why am I grieving?" but rather, "What do I do now?" Without grief there can be no recovery. At the same time, continuing in grief can be just as unhealthy.

There's no perfect pattern or timetable. Everyone experiences grief in different ways.

Years ago Granger Westberg, a pastor and hospital chaplain, wrote a little book called *Good Grief.* In this "faith-based guide to understanding and healing," Westberg discusses the ten stages of grief he has observed in people, whether they had lost a loved one or a job. The stages are for anyone working through a loss of their own or in the life of a friend or loved one.[3]

Stage One: The Shock. If there's one stage common to everyone who experiences loss, it's the shock of realizing that the person or thing they love is no longer there. Like a jolt of electricity, a shock wakes us up to reality.

Stage Two: Emotion. Shock gives way to emotion. Some people hold their emotions in for a while, and that's okay—as long as the backup doesn't last beyond what is healthy. If you're not used to crying and perhaps consider it a sign of weakness, remember how King David wept over the loss of his son.

Stage Three: Loneliness. Even if you are surrounded by loved ones, your loss will eventually lead to loneliness and possibly depression.

In wintertime in the Central Valley of California, it's common for a thick layer of fog to block out the sun for days and sometimes weeks on end. If you stay too long in the fog without seeing the sun, depression can set in. Of course, people who live in central California know that a drive to the mountains is all it takes to rise above the fog and feel the warmth of the winter sun. In the same way, if depression has set in, you can look to the one who made the mountains.

> *I look up to the mountains—does my help come from there? My help comes from the LORD, who made the heavens and the earth!* PSALM 121:1–2

Stage Four: Distress. Sometimes grief can lead to real physical distress. Treatment may require more than medication. You may need to evaluate those things that are worth living for: children, grandchildren, friends, another worthy cause. Distress can be overcome by stressing what's important.

Stage Five: Panic. Westberg writes that panic comes from the fear of the unknown. And our minds may play tricks on us. It's common for people who have lost a limb to feel a sensation of the missing arm or leg still being there. When we know that panic is related to what is no longer there, we can deal with it.

Stage Six: Guilt. Sometimes partners or friends of one who has died feel guilt, even if they did nothing to contribute to the loss. The apostle Peter felt horrible guilt after denying Christ three times on the eve of His crucifixion. After Jesus came back to life, He comforted Peter and gave him an assignment: "If you love me, take care of my sheep" (see John 21:16). Peter needed to look beyond his guilt to the greater need.

Stage Seven: Anger. How often have you known people who got angry at the ones who left them? It happens more often than you may realize. Perhaps it's happened to you. Perhaps you're mad at God. That's okay. He can handle it. Give your anger to Him.

Stage Eight: Resistance. Just as you get close to breaking through your grief, you may have a tendency to resist. Grief can become a kind of morbid friend, a crutch. If you know people stuck in this stage, help pull them out. All it takes is compassion and encouragement.

Stage Nine: Hope. Ah, finally, after months or maybe years, hope does break through, like the sun after a prolonged rain. Life does go on. A smile will return. God does care.

Stage Ten: Faith. Just because hope eventually returns doesn't mean it can't fade again. All of us—whether we're grieving or just going through ordinary hard stuff—need to keep our eyes focused on God. When we focus on the storm rather than the Master of the sea, we will eventually sink. We must have faith that our gracious God will hold us by the hand and see us through our struggles.

. . .In the Hard Stuff

- A grieving heart is a loving heart.

- Helping someone through the grieving process is one of the greatest gifts you can give.

- The only way to get yourself out of the fog is to rise above it.

- Like a houseguest who stays too long, grief that lingers can become a real nuisance. Know when to show grief the door.

- God is the only one who can get us through the stages of grief—because He is the only one who can give us hope.

It should be a pleasure to those that have their home
in the other world to think of being "no more in this world";
for when we have done what we have to do in this world. . .
what is there that should court our stay?
When we receive a sentence of death within ourselves,
with a holy triumph we should say. . .
"now I shall wander no more in this howling wilderness,
be tossed no more on this stormy sea;
now I am no more in this world,
but can cheerfully quit it and give it a final farewell."

Matthew Henry

THIRTY-EIGHT

AFRAID TO DEATH OF DYING

Woody Allen once said, "I'm not afraid of death. I just don't want to be around when it happens." Most of us feel the same way. Our own mortality is something that we'd prefer not to confront. So we put off preparing a will, and we don't talk with our families about funeral and burial arrangements. Even when faced with terminal illness, many families discuss generic pleasantries and avoid the emotional issues that accompany death. We simply do not want to think about what happens when we're gone.

But what are we so afraid of? Though it sounds ironic, death is a natural part of life. It will happen to everyone. It has already happened to people we know and love. Since it's so commonplace, why is there still such an apprehension of death?

Despite its pervasive presence in our world, death remains shrouded in mystery:

- *For each of us, it is a first-time experience.* Although others have gone through it, we haven't. Thus, we can't predict our feelings and emotional responses. Until it happens, we don't know how we will respond. Will we show bravery or cowardice?

- *For most of us, we don't know the circumstances.* Will our death be the result of an accident which ends our life quickly and unexpectedly? Or will our dying process be painful and prolonged due to a debilitating disease? Will we die with dignity or in circumstances we consider humiliating?

- *For all of us, we have regrets.* Because each of us is far from perfect, life is a trail of decisions, mistakes, and actions we would prefer to "do over." There are relationships that didn't end well, and goals left unaccomplished. We know that death not only terminates our life but also any possibility of concluding some of our unfinished business.

- *For all of us, there are those we leave behind.* It is not egotistical to acknowledge that family members and friends will mourn your death. Your quality relationship with them is revealed by your concern that they will experience sorrow at your passing. You don't want them to have to experience the grief associated with your death.

- *For everyone else, life will go on.* Although death brings finality to our lives, the rest of the world will continue living. This may cause us mixed emotions. We are glad for our survivors, but we realize that we are relatively dispensable in the large scheme of things. If life can go on without us, we question whether we were ever really needed.

It's no wonder that death causes apprehension if we focus myopically on all the unknowns. The negative symptoms of such a perspective can be reversed, however, if we approach death with our actual knowledge of life after death. For those who love God and have followed Him in life, death is the starting point of an eternal life characterized by:

- the presence of God Himself;
- the absence of evil;
- no pain and suffering;
- a whole and healthy spiritual body free of any defect or deformity;
- a reunion with others; and
- an eternal state of happiness, peace, and love.

Death is to be dreaded if we associate it only with the past and what is unknown. But death can be approached boldly and with anticipation if we view it in the context of our relationship with God. Our attitude about death is determined by our perspective: Are we looking down at the world or up to heaven? This choice of perspective was articulated well by British theologian Austin Farrer:

> When we [have died and are in heaven], *and look back on earthly life, we shall not see it as a vigorous battlefield from which we have gracefully retired; we shall view it as an insubstantial dream from which we have happily awoken.*

When you are confronted with death, don't look back with regret or ahead with anxiety. Rejoice in the eternal life that awaits those who love God. According to His plan, your best is yet to come.

. . .In the Hard Stuff

- You can't avoid death—but during this life you can make arrangements for how you will spend eternity.

- Some people love life so much, they would prefer to live forever without death. Others love God so much they don't fear death.

- Considering the consequences of death may change your attitudes and actions in life.

- In may be inappropriate to wish for death, but everyone should long for heaven.

- Death may take you out of sight, but it doesn't take you out of being.

F or I do not seek to understand
in order that I may believe,
but I believe in order that I may understand.

Anselm of Canterbury

THIRTY-NINE

BELIEVING GOD

It's one thing to believe in God. The evidence for His existence is so overwhelming—from the vast wonders of the heavens to the intricate marvels of DNA—that it truly takes more faith to believe the universe occurred by chance than it does to believe in an all-powerful and all-loving Creator. Even the demons believe in God (James 2:19), so don't put too much stock in simple *belief.*

What matters more than a belief in God's *existence* is a belief in God's *words.* To put it another way, it's not enough just to believe *in* God; you must also believe *Him.*

This is so important because God has given specific instructions on how to establish a meaningful relationship with Him. We don't get right with God by being good people, because no one is good enough. We get right with God by receiving the goodness of Jesus on our behalf (see John 3:16). We can disagree with God's words and His methods all we want, but that doesn't count—because God isn't debating us. If God exists, the only thing that counts is what He says.

Believing God is crucial to this whole business of life's hard stuff. If God is just some being we've created to make ourselves feel better, then what He says isn't all that important. But if He is the One who made us, we can believe what He has promised—both for now and forever.

Many believers struggle in this area. They wonder if God is capable of making good on His promises to save, protect, and preserve us for all eternity. As a result, they lead insecure and troubled lives, never quite sure that God is both interested in and capable of taking care of them. Jesus knew this weakness of ours, so He addressed it specifically:

> *"So don't worry about having enough food or drink
> or clothing. Why be like the pagans who are so deeply*

concerned about these things? Your heavenly Father
already knows all your needs, and he will give you all
you need from day to day if you live for him and make
the Kingdom of God your primary concern."

MATTHEW 6:31–33

There you have it. We don't need to worry about our daily needs. God is there in the small, everyday stuff like food, shelter, and clothing. All He asks is that we give Him first place in our lives.

Then, to assure us that He's also in the hard stuff, God gives this promise:

And I am convinced that nothing can ever separate us
from his love. Death can't, and life can't. The angels
can't, and the demons can't. Our fears for today, our
worries about tomorrow, and even the powers of hell
can't keep God's love away. Whether we are high above
the sky or in the deepest ocean, nothing in all creation
will ever be able to separate us from the love of God
that is revealed in Christ Jesus our Lord.

ROMANS 8:38–39

You can believe God to make good on His promises to bring you through the hard stuff. And you can believe God when He says He will never let you go.

- Believing in God is a great place to start—but it must never be the end.

- There is the God who is, and there is the God we want. They are not always the same.

- Making the Kingdom of God your primary concern means you prioritize your life around God and His will for you.

- Putting God in second place will never do. If God isn't your first priority, you might as well take Him off your list.

- We may let go of God, but He will never let go of us.

I heard a loud shout from the throne, saying,
"Look, the home of God is now among his people!
He will live with them, and they will be his people.
God himself will be with them.
He will remove all of their sorrows,
and there will be no more death or sorrow or crying or pain.
For the old world and its evils are gone forever."

Revelation 21:3–4

FORTY

THE HOPE OF HEAVEN

Do you have a favorite place where you can escape the cares and worries of this world? Do you long to visit some exotic and beautiful spot you've seen in magazines or on the travel channel, hoping to be transported to a state of peace, serenity, and wonder?

This desire to experience the beauty and restorative power of the Creator's handiwork is a gift from our great God. The earth has problems, but its delights far outweigh the disasters. Still, as wonderful as it is, our world now is but a shadow of the world to come. Earth may be a home ideally suited for human survival and even enjoyment—but heaven will be a perfect dwelling place with riches and wonders that exceed our imaginative ability.

Do you believe in heaven? Most people do, but only on a *wishing* level. They *hope* heaven exists, if for no other reason than that it hints at a world better than this one. Yes, heaven offers eternal life infinitely better than the temporary life we have now, but we don't have to *wish* it to be true. You can believe by faith that heaven is a real place, where there will be no more death or sorrow or crying or pain.

> *What is faith? It is the confident assurance that what we hope for is going to happen. It is the evidence of things we cannot yet see.* HEBREWS 11:1

If you believe God exists and you believe what He says, you can have real hope that there is a real place called heaven, created by God to last forever. Heaven is where Jesus lives now (Acts 3:21), and where those who have trusted Jesus will live in the future (John 14:2). True believers will see Jesus face-to-face in heaven. In fact, believers will be *glorified*—that is, raised up with Jesus, seated and exalted with Him in heaven (Ephesians 2:6). You won't be sitting on a cloud strumming a harp in heaven. You will worship God and enjoy every blessing imaginable.

The psalmist David noted several qualities of God that will be magnified in heaven. First, you will experience total, wonderful, blissful *peace* because God will care for your every need:

> *The LORD is my shepherd; I have everything I need.*
> *He lets me rest in green meadows; he leads me beside*
> *peaceful streams.* PSALM 23:1–2

You will also have complete *rest*, because God will remove all of your burdens:

> *Those who live in the shelter of the Most High will*
> *find rest in the shadow of the Almighty.*
> PSALM 91:1

You will have absolute *security*, protected from harm of any kind:

> *This I declare of the LORD: He alone is my refuge, my*
> *place of safety; he is my God, and I am trusting him.*
> PSALM 91:2

And you will experience the incomparable *beauty* of God's incredible paradise that will be yours to explore and enjoy endlessly:

> *The heavens tell of the glory of God. The skies display*
> *his marvelous craftsmanship.*　　　PSALM 19:1

Amidst the trouble and turbulence of our world, the hope of heaven is a future reality that can give us a present assurance. Some day we will be ushered into the eternal home of our dreams—a home of everlasting peace, rest, security, and beauty.

- Knowing that heaven waits for us in the future gives us a reason for hope now.

- Heaven isn't a fairy-tale place in the sky; it's the home of the one true God. And someday we will share that home with Him.

- Anyone who has a relationship with God has already experienced a taste of heaven.

- Anything we taste of heaven now will become a feast in eternity.

- The gates of heaven are open to anyone who will open their heart to God.

I know not what the future holds,
but I know who holds the future.

Ira F. Stanphill

FORTY-ONE

GOD IS IN THE HARD STUFF

Just saying the phrase *God is in the hard stuff* doesn't make the hard stuff easier to endure. We are the first to admit that those six words are not a spiritual mantra that will make your difficult circumstances vanish—or even diminish. Just as saying "think thin and you'll be thin" will not shed unwanted pounds, neither will repeating the words "God is in the hard stuff" relieve the pain and problems of your difficult circumstances.

We can imagine that these words are hollow to anyone in the midst of pain, suffering, and discouragement. Even the perspectives we have given in the preceding chapters may not seem immediately helpful. You might even wonder, "What good is God?"

after reading the previous chapters:

- When we said *God never intends to insulate you from problems,* you may have heard: "God doesn't keep trouble from happening."
- When we said *God can use difficult circumstances to make you a better person,* you may have heard: "God won't make it hurt any less."
- And when we said *God will be with you all the way until it ends,* you may have thought: "Yeah, but He doesn't make it end any quicker."

Sometimes the pain is so great you can't appreciate the long-range benefit of God's involvement. So let's deal with your very honest and understandable question: "What good is God?"

There is one immediate benefit to recognizing God is with you in the midst of your problems. It is what you need the most if you are going to hold up under the pressure of your adversity—peace.

Isn't that ironic? God promises to deliver the emotion that is completely contrary to the reaction the circumstances cause:

- When you feel pain—God promises peace.
- When you are living in fear—God promises peace.
- When you have unbearable stress—God promises peace.
- When you are brokenhearted with grief—God promises peace.
- When you are depressed and discouraged—God promises peace.

It just doesn't make sense, does it? How is peace possible in circumstances characterized by death, pain, danger, fear, and loss? Humanly speaking, peace is impossible in such situations. But with God, we aren't talking about *human* peace. We are dealing with a supernatural peace that is experienced only through knowing God. Here is how the Bible describes it:

> *Don't worry about anything; instead, pray about everything. Tell God what you need, and thank him for all he has done. If you do this, you will experience God's peace, which is far more wonderful than the human mind can understand. His peace will guard your hearts and minds as you live in Christ Jesus.* PHILIPPIANS 4:6–7

We won't attempt to define this kind of peace. As the Bible says, it is spiritually understood in the midst of your struggles. This peace—which surpasses our human understanding—doesn't make the problems go away. That's precisely why we need to experience it during those difficult times. And this supernatural peace will not always make things easier in the ways you might hope:

- It won't repair a broken marriage.
- It won't cure the cancer.
- It won't replenish the bank account.
- It won't bring anyone back from the dead.

But it will make life better in ways that you can't imagine:

- You will feel God's presence.
- You will begin to see with God's perspective.
- You will hear God's voice.
- You will sense God's love.

And these things—despite the surrounding problems and suffering—will make life good.

- God's peace doesn't remove us from the world, but it makes living in the world possible.

- You'll feel God's peace only when you allow Him to be in charge of your problems.

- With God in the hard stuff, His peace is there, too.

- God's peace can keep you from going to pieces.

- God doesn't offer us a life filled with peaceful pursuits. But He offers a peaceful life in a hard world.

ENDNOTES

[1] Walt Russell, *"Facing the Pain of Dementia,"* Biola Connections (Summer 2004), 16–17.

[2] Mother Teresa, "Prayers," *Mother Teresa: The Path of Love* Homesite [online] (accessed April 1, 2004); available from http://home.Comcast.net/~motherteresasite/prayers.html; Internet.

[3] Granger F. Westberg, *Good Grief* (Minneapolis: Augsburg Fortress Press, 1997).

ABOUT THE AUTHORS

Bruce Bickel is a lawyer and Stan Jantz is a marketing consultant. They have collaborated on more than fifty books with combined sales of more than three million copies. Their passion is to present biblical truth in a correct, clear, and casual manner that encourages people to connect in a meaningful way with the living God.

Contact Bruce & Stan at:
www.christianity101online.com